3277

THIS IS YOUR **PASSBOOK**® FOR ...

HIGH PRESSURE PLANT TENDER

NATIONAL LEARNING CORPORATION®

passbooks.com

Copyright © 2018 by

National Learning Corporation

212 Michael Drive, Syosset, NY 11791
(516) 921-8888 • www.passbooks.com
E-mail: info@passbooks.com

PUBLISHED IN THE UNITED STATES OF AMERICA

PASSBOOK® SERIES

THE *PASSBOOK® SERIES* has been created to prepare applicants and candidates for the ultimate academic battlefield – the examination room.

At some time in our lives, each and every one of us may be required to take an examination – for validation, matriculation, admission, qualification, registration, certification, or licensure.

Based on the assumption that every applicant or candidate has met the basic formal educational standards, has taken the required number of courses, and read the necessary texts, the *PASSBOOK® SERIES* furnishes the one special preparation which may assure passing with confidence, instead of failing with insecurity. Examination questions – together with answers – are furnished as the basic vehicle for study so that the mysteries of the examination and its compounding difficulties may be eliminated or diminished by a sure method.

This book is meant to help you pass your examination provided that you qualify and are serious in your objective.

The entire field is reviewed through the huge store of content information which is succinctly presented through a provocative and challenging approach – the question-and-answer method.

A climate of success is established by furnishing the correct answers at the end of each test.

You soon learn to recognize types of questions, forms of questions, and patterns of questioning. You may even begin to anticipate expected outcomes.

You perceive that many questions are repeated or adapted so that you can gain acute insights, which may enable you to score many sure points.

You learn how to confront new questions, or types of questions, and to attack them confidently and work out the correct answers.

You note objectives and emphases, and recognize pitfalls and dangers, so that you may make positive educational adjustments.

Moreover, you are kept fully informed in relation to new concepts, methods, practices, and directions in the field.

You discover that you arre actually taking the examination all the time: you are preparing for the examination by "taking" an examination, not by reading extraneous and/or supererogatory textbooks.

In short, this PASSBOOK®, used directedly, should be an important factor in helping you to pass your test.

HIGH PRESSURE PLANT TENDER

DUTIES;

High Pressure Plant Tenders under direct supervision, tend oil, gas or coal of this equipment. They may be assigned to inspect, maintain and repair heating, ventilation, refrigeration, air conditioning and related auxiliary systems and equipment. They hand fire high-pressure boilers using solid fuels, and stoker equipment and incinerator furnaces using burnable refuse; clean fires; tend and operate stoker equipment, oil-, gas-, or coal-fired high-pressure boilers and incinerator furnaces, and related equipment; maintain, clean, repair and assist in the inspection and testing of high-pressure boilers, incinerators, auxiliaries and related equipment; maintain, clean, repair and/or tend to, and assist in the inspection and testing of equipment and systems used in heating, ventilation, refrigeration, air conditioning and related auxiliary equipment, such as cooling towers, air handlers, chilled water pumps, air cleaners and filters, fans, heat exchangers, tubes, air treatment assemblies, humidifiers/dehumidifiers, and controls; may dismantle and/or assemble equipment associated with heating, ventilation, refrigeration, air conditioning and mechanical systems to make it operational; requisition parts as required; and may operate a motor vehicle. All High Pressure Plant Tenders perform related work.

SCOPE OF THE EXAMINATION

The multiple-choice test is designed to assess the extent to which candidates have certain knowledge abilities determined to be important to the performance of the tasks of a High Pressure Plant Tender. Task categories to be tested are as follows: operation, maintenance and repair of high-pressure boilers, pumps, and related auxiliary equipment; inspection and testing of high-pressure boilers and related auxiliary equipment; and administrative duties.

The multiple-choice test may include questions on the operation and maintenance of high pressure boilers including burner, ignition, controls, valves, pumps, meters, gauges and regulators; operation and maintenance of auxiliaries and refrigeration equipment; selection and usage of lubricants, packing and gaskets; use of appropriate tools, instruments and lubricating devices; safety; and other related areas including number facility, written comprehension, and written expression.

HOW TO TAKE A TEST

I. YOU MUST PASS AN EXAMINATION

A. *WHAT EVERY CANDIDATE SHOULD KNOW*

Examination applicants often ask us for help in preparing for the written test. What can I study in advance? What kinds of questions will be asked? How will the test be given? How will the papers be graded?

As an applicant for a civil service examination, you may be wondering about some of these things. Our purpose here is to suggest effective methods of advance study and to describe civil service examinations.

Your chances for success on this examination can be increased if you know how to prepare. Those "pre-examination jitters" can be reduced if you know what to expect. You can even experience an adventure in good citizenship if you know why civil service exams are given.

B. *WHY ARE CIVIL SERVICE EXAMINATIONS GIVEN?*

Civil service examinations are important to you in two ways. As a citizen, you want public jobs filled by employees who know how to do their work. As a job seeker, you want a fair chance to compete for that job on an equal footing with other candidates. The best-known means of accomplishing this two-fold goal is the competitive examination.

Exams are widely publicized throughout the nation. They may be administered for jobs in federal, state, city, municipal, town or village governments or agencies.

Any citizen may apply, with some limitations, such as the age or residence of applicants. Your experience and education may be reviewed to see whether you meet the requirements for the particular examination. When these requirements exist, they are reasonable and applied consistently to all applicants. Thus, a competitive examination may cause you some uneasiness now, but it is your privilege and safeguard.

C. *HOW ARE CIVIL SERVICE EXAMS DEVELOPED?*

Examinations are carefully written by trained technicians who are specialists in the field known as "psychological measurement," in consultation with recognized authorities in the field of work that the test will cover. These experts recommend the subject matter areas or skills to be tested; only those knowledges or skills important to your success on the job are included. The most reliable books and source materials available are used as references. Together, the experts and technicians judge the difficulty level of the questions.

Test technicians know how to phrase questions so that the problem is clearly stated. Their ethics do not permit "trick" or "catch" questions. Questions may have been tried out on sample groups, or subjected to statistical analysis, to determine their usefulness.

Written tests are often used in combination with performance tests, ratings of training and experience, and oral interviews. All of these measures combine to form the best-known means of finding the right person for the right job.

II. HOW TO PASS THE WRITTEN TEST

A. NATURE OF THE EXAMINATION

To prepare intelligently for civil service examinations, you should know how they differ from school examinations you have taken. In school you were assigned certain definite pages to read or subjects to cover. The examination questions were quite detailed and usually emphasized memory. Civil service exams, on the other hand, try to discover your present ability to perform the duties of a position, plus your potentiality to learn these duties. In other words, a civil service exam attempts to predict how successful you will be. Questions cover such a broad area that they cannot be as minute and detailed as school exam questions.

In the public service similar kinds of work, or positions, are grouped together in one "class." This process is known as *position-classification*. All the positions in a class are paid according to the salary range for that class. One class title covers all of these positions, and they are all tested by the same examination.

B. FOUR BASIC STEPS

1) Study the announcement

How, then, can you know what subjects to study? Our best answer is: "Learn as much as possible about the class of positions for which you've applied." The exam will test the knowledge, skills and abilities needed to do the work.

Your most valuable source of information about the position you want is the official exam announcement. This announcement lists the training and experience qualifications. Check these standards and apply only if you come reasonably close to meeting them.

The brief description of the position in the examination announcement offers some clues to the subjects which will be tested. Think about the job itself. Review the duties in your mind. Can you perform them, or are there some in which you are rusty? Fill in the blank spots in your preparation.

Many jurisdictions preview the written test in the exam announcement by including a section called "Knowledge and Abilities Required," "Scope of the Examination," or some similar heading. Here you will find out specifically what fields will be tested.

2) Review your own background

Once you learn in general what the position is all about, and what you need to know to do the work, ask yourself which subjects you already know fairly well and which need improvement. You may wonder whether to concentrate on improving your strong areas or on building some background in your fields of weakness. When the announcement has specified "some knowledge" or "considerable knowledge," or has used adjectives like "beginning principles of…" or "advanced … methods," you can get a clue as to the number and difficulty of questions to be asked in any given field. More questions, and hence broader coverage, would be included for those subjects which are more important in the work. Now weigh your strengths and weaknesses against the job requirements and prepare accordingly.

3) Determine the level of the position

Another way to tell how intensively you should prepare is to understand the level of the job for which you are applying. Is it the entering level? In other words, is this the position in which beginners in a field of work are hired? Or is it an intermediate or advanced level? Sometimes this is indicated by such words as "Junior" or "Senior" in the class title. Other jurisdictions use Roman numerals to designate the level – Clerk I, Clerk II, for example. The word "Supervisor" sometimes appears in the title. If the level is not indicated by the title, check the description of duties. Will you be working under very close supervision, or will you have responsibility for independent decisions in this work?

4) Choose appropriate study materials

Now that you know the subjects to be examined and the relative amount of each subject to be covered, you can choose suitable study materials. For beginning level jobs, or even advanced ones, if you have a pronounced weakness in some aspect of your training, read a modern, standard textbook in that field. Be sure it is up to date and has general coverage. Such books are normally available at your library, and the librarian will be glad to help you locate one. For entry-level positions, questions of appropriate difficulty are chosen – neither highly advanced questions, nor those too simple. Such questions require careful thought but not advanced training.

If the position for which you are applying is technical or advanced, you will read more advanced, specialized material. If you are already familiar with the basic principles of your field, elementary textbooks would waste your time. Concentrate on advanced textbooks and technical periodicals. Think through the concepts and review difficult problems in your field.

These are all general sources. You can get more ideas on your own initiative, following these leads. For example, training manuals and publications of the government agency which employs workers in your field can be useful, particularly for technical and professional positions. A letter or visit to the government department involved may result in more specific study suggestions, and certainly will provide you with a more definite idea of the exact nature of the position you are seeking.

III. KINDS OF TESTS

Tests are used for purposes other than measuring knowledge and ability to perform specified duties. For some positions, it is equally important to test ability to make adjustments to new situations or to profit from training. In others, basic mental abilities not dependent on information are essential. Questions which test these things may not appear as pertinent to the duties of the position as those which test for knowledge and information. Yet they are often highly important parts of a fair examination. For very general questions, it is almost impossible to help you direct your study efforts. What we can do is to point out some of the more common of these general abilities needed in public service positions and describe some typical questions.

1) General information

Broad, general information has been found useful for predicting job success in some kinds of work. This is tested in a variety of ways, from vocabulary lists to questions about current events. Basic background in some field of work, such as sociology or economics, may be sampled in a group of questions. Often these are principles which have become familiar to most persons through exposure rather than through formal training. It is difficult to advise you how to study for these questions; being alert to the world around you is our best suggestion.

2) Verbal ability

An example of an ability needed in many positions is verbal or language ability. Verbal ability is, in brief, the ability to use and understand words. Vocabulary and grammar tests are typical measures of this ability. Reading comprehension or paragraph interpretation questions are common in many kinds of civil service tests. You are given a paragraph of written material and asked to find its central meaning.

3) Numerical ability

Number skills can be tested by the familiar arithmetic problem, by checking paired lists of numbers to see which are alike and which are different, or by interpreting charts and graphs. In the latter test, a graph may be printed in the test booklet which you are asked to use as the basis for answering questions.

4) Observation

A popular test for law-enforcement positions is the observation test. A picture is shown to you for several minutes, then taken away. Questions about the picture test your ability to observe both details and larger elements.

5) Following directions

In many positions in the public service, the employee must be able to carry out written instructions dependably and accurately. You may be given a chart with several columns, each column listing a variety of information. The questions require you to carry out directions involving the information given in the chart.

6) Skills and aptitudes

Performance tests effectively measure some manual skills and aptitudes. When the skill is one in which you are trained, such as typing or shorthand, you can practice. These tests are often very much like those given in business school or high school courses. For many of the other skills and aptitudes, however, no short-time preparation can be made. Skills and abilities natural to you or that you have developed throughout your lifetime are being tested.

Many of the general questions just described provide all the data needed to answer the questions and ask you to use your reasoning ability to find the answers. Your best preparation for these tests, as well as for tests of facts and ideas, is to be at your physical and mental best. You, no doubt, have your own methods of getting into an exam-taking mood and keeping "in shape." The next section lists some ideas on this subject.

IV. KINDS OF QUESTIONS

Only rarely is the "essay" question, which you answer in narrative form, used in civil service tests. Civil service tests are usually of the short-answer type. Full instructions for answering these questions will be given to you at the examination. But in case this is your first experience with short-answer questions and separate answer sheets, here is what you need to know:

1) Multiple-choice Questions

Most popular of the short-answer questions is the "multiple choice" or "best answer" question. It can be used, for example, to test for factual knowledge, ability to solve problems or judgment in meeting situations found at work.

A multiple-choice question is normally one of three types—

- It can begin with an incomplete statement followed by several possible endings. You are to find the one ending which *best* completes the statement, although some of the others may not be entirely wrong.
- It can also be a complete statement in the form of a question which is answered by choosing one of the statements listed.
- It can be in the form of a problem – again you select the best answer.

Here is an example of a multiple-choice question with a discussion which should give you some clues as to the method for choosing the right answer:

When an employee has a complaint about his assignment, the action which will *best* help him overcome his difficulty is to
   A. discuss his difficulty with his coworkers
   B. take the problem to the head of the organization
   C. take the problem to the person who gave him the assignment
   D. say nothing to anyone about his complaint

In answering this question, you should study each of the choices to find which is best. Consider choice "A" – Certainly an employee may discuss his complaint with fellow employees, but no change or improvement can result, and the complaint remains unresolved. Choice "B" is a poor choice since the head of the organization probably does not know what assignment you have been given, and taking your problem to him is known as "going over the head" of the supervisor. The supervisor, or person who made the assignment, is the person who can clarify it or correct any injustice. Choice "C" is, therefore, correct. To say nothing, as in choice "D," is unwise. Supervisors have and interest in knowing the problems employees are facing, and the employee is seeking a solution to his problem.

2) True/False Questions

The "true/false" or "right/wrong" form of question is sometimes used. Here a complete statement is given. Your job is to decide whether the statement is right or wrong.

SAMPLE: A roaming cell-phone call to a nearby city costs less than a non-roaming call to a distant city.

This statement is wrong, or false, since roaming calls are more expensive.
This is not a complete list of all possible question forms, although most of the others are variations of these common types. You will always get complete directions for

answering questions. Be sure you understand *how* to mark your answers – ask questions until you do.

V. RECORDING YOUR ANSWERS

Computer terminals are used more and more today for many different kinds of exams.

For an examination with very few applicants, you may be told to record your answers in the test booklet itself. Separate answer sheets are much more common. If this separate answer sheet is to be scored by machine – and this is often the case – it is highly important that you mark your answers correctly in order to get credit.

An electronic scoring machine is often used in civil service offices because of the speed with which papers can be scored. Machine-scored answer sheets must be marked with a pencil, which will be given to you. This pencil has a high graphite content which responds to the electronic scoring machine. As a matter of fact, stray dots may register as answers, so do not let your pencil rest on the answer sheet while you are pondering the correct answer. Also, if your pencil lead breaks or is otherwise defective, ask for another.

Since the answer sheet will be dropped in a slot in the scoring machine, be careful not to bend the corners or get the paper crumpled.

The answer sheet normally has five vertical columns of numbers, with 30 numbers to a column. These numbers correspond to the question numbers in your test booklet. After each number, going across the page are four or five pairs of dotted lines. These short dotted lines have small letters or numbers above them. The first two pairs may also have a "T" or "F" above the letters. This indicates that the first two pairs only are to be used if the questions are of the true-false type. If the questions are multiple choice, disregard the "T" and "F" and pay attention only to the small letters or numbers.

Answer your questions in the manner of the sample that follows:

32. The largest city in the United States is
    A. Washington, D.C.
    B. New York City
    C. Chicago
    D. Detroit
    E. San Francisco

1) Choose the answer you think is best. (New York City is the largest, so "B" is correct.)
2) Find the row of dotted lines numbered the same as the question you are answering. (Find row number 32)
3) Find the pair of dotted lines corresponding to the answer. (Find the pair of lines under the mark "B.")
4) Make a solid black mark between the dotted lines.

VI. BEFORE THE TEST

Common sense will help you find procedures to follow to get ready for an examination. Too many of us, however, overlook these sensible measures. Indeed, nervousness and fatigue have been found to be the most serious reasons why applicants fail to do their best on civil service tests. Here is a list of reminders:

- Begin your preparation early – Don't wait until the last minute to go scurrying around for books and materials or to find out what the position is all about.
- Prepare continuously – An hour a night for a week is better than an all-night cram session. This has been definitely established. What is more, a night a week for a month will return better dividends than crowding your study into a shorter period of time.
- Locate the place of the exam – You have been sent a notice telling you when and where to report for the examination. If the location is in a different town or otherwise unfamiliar to you, it would be well to inquire the best route and learn something about the building.
- Relax the night before the test – Allow your mind to rest. Do not study at all that night. Plan some mild recreation or diversion; then go to bed early and get a good night's sleep.
- Get up early enough to make a leisurely trip to the place for the test – This way unforeseen events, traffic snarls, unfamiliar buildings, etc. will not upset you.
- Dress comfortably – A written test is not a fashion show. You will be known by number and not by name, so wear something comfortable.
- Leave excess paraphernalia at home – Shopping bags and odd bundles will get in your way. You need bring only the items mentioned in the official notice you received; usually everything you need is provided. Do not bring reference books to the exam. They will only confuse those last minutes and be taken away from you when in the test room.
- Arrive somewhat ahead of time – If because of transportation schedules you must get there very early, bring a newspaper or magazine to take your mind off yourself while waiting.
- Locate the examination room – When you have found the proper room, you will be directed to the seat or part of the room where you will sit. Sometimes you are given a sheet of instructions to read while you are waiting. Do not fill out any forms until you are told to do so; just read them and be prepared.
- Relax and prepare to listen to the instructions
- If you have any physical problem that may keep you from doing your best, be sure to tell the test administrator. If you are sick or in poor health, you really cannot do your best on the exam. You can come back and take the test some other time.

VII. AT THE TEST

The day of the test is here and you have the test booklet in your hand. The temptation to get going is very strong. Caution! There is more to success than knowing the right answers. You must know how to identify your papers and understand variations in the type of short-answer question used in this particular examination. Follow these suggestions for maximum results from your efforts:

1) Cooperate with the monitor

The test administrator has a duty to create a situation in which you can be as much at ease as possible. He will give instructions, tell you when to begin, check to see that you are marking your answer sheet correctly, and so on. He is not there to guard you, although he will see that your competitors do not take unfair advantage. He wants to help you do your best.

2) Listen to all instructions

Don't jump the gun! Wait until you understand all directions. In most civil service tests you get more time than you need to answer the questions. So don't be in a hurry. Read each word of instructions until you clearly understand the meaning. Study the examples, listen to all announcements and follow directions. Ask questions if you do not understand what to do.

3) Identify your papers

Civil service exams are usually identified by number only. You will be assigned a number; you must not put your name on your test papers. Be sure to copy your number correctly. Since more than one exam may be given, copy your exact examination title.

4) Plan your time

Unless you are told that a test is a "speed" or "rate of work" test, speed itself is usually not important. Time enough to answer all the questions will be provided, but this does not mean that you have all day. An overall time limit has been set. Divide the total time (in minutes) by the number of questions to determine the approximate time you have for each question.

5) Do not linger over difficult questions

If you come across a difficult question, mark it with a paper clip (useful to have along) and come back to it when you have been through the booklet. One caution if you do this – be sure to skip a number on your answer sheet as well. Check often to be sure that you have not lost your place and that you are marking in the row numbered the same as the question you are answering.

6) Read the questions

Be sure you know what the question asks! Many capable people are unsuccessful because they failed to *read* the questions correctly.

7) Answer all questions

Unless you have been instructed that a penalty will be deducted for incorrect answers, it is better to guess than to omit a question.

8) Speed tests

It is often better NOT to guess on speed tests. It has been found that on timed tests people are tempted to spend the last few seconds before time is called in marking answers at random – without even reading them – in the hope of picking up a few extra points. To discourage this practice, the instructions may warn you that your score will be "corrected" for guessing. That is, a penalty will be applied. The incorrect answers will be deducted from the correct ones, or some other penalty formula will be used.

9) Review your answers

If you finish before time is called, go back to the questions you guessed or omitted to give them further thought. Review other answers if you have time.

10) Return your test materials

If you are ready to leave before others have finished or time is called, take ALL your materials to the monitor and leave quietly. Never take any test material with you. The monitor can discover whose papers are not complete, and taking a test booklet may be grounds for disqualification.

VIII. EXAMINATION TECHNIQUES

1) Read the general instructions carefully. These are usually printed on the first page of the exam booklet. As a rule, these instructions refer to the timing of the examination; the fact that you should not start work until the signal and must stop work at a signal, etc. If there are any *special* instructions, such as a choice of questions to be answered, make sure that you note this instruction carefully.

2) When you are ready to start work on the examination, that is as soon as the signal has been given, read the instructions to each question booklet, underline any key words or phrases, such as *least, best, outline, describe* and the like. In this way you will tend to answer as requested rather than discover on reviewing your paper that you *listed without describing*, that you selected the *worst* choice rather than the *best* choice, etc.

3) If the examination is of the objective or multiple-choice type – that is, each question will also give a series of possible answers: A, B, C or D, and you are called upon to select the best answer and write the letter next to that answer on your answer paper – it is advisable to start answering each question in turn. There may be anywhere from 50 to 100 such questions in the three or four hours allotted and you can see how much time would be taken if you read through all the questions before beginning to answer any. Furthermore, if you come across a question or group of questions which you know would be difficult to answer, it would undoubtedly affect your handling of all the other questions.

4) If the examination is of the essay type and contains but a few questions, it is a moot point as to whether you should read all the questions before starting to answer any one. Of course, if you are given a choice – say five out of seven and the like – then it is essential to read all the questions so you can eliminate the two that are most difficult. If, however, you are asked to answer all the questions, there may be danger in trying to answer the easiest one first because you may find that you will spend too much time on it. The best technique is to answer the first question, then proceed to the second, etc.

5) Time your answers. Before the exam begins, write down the time it started, then add the time allowed for the examination and write down the time it must be completed, then divide the time available somewhat as follows:

- If 3-1/2 hours are allowed, that would be 210 minutes. If you have 80 objective-type questions, that would be an average of 2-1/2 minutes per question. Allow yourself no more than 2 minutes per question, or a total of 160 minutes, which will permit about 50 minutes to review.
- If for the time allotment of 210 minutes there are 7 essay questions to answer, that would average about 30 minutes a question. Give yourself only 25 minutes per question so that you have about 35 minutes to review.

6) The most important instruction is to *read each question* and make sure you know what is wanted. The second most important instruction is to *time yourself properly* so that you answer every question. The third most important instruction is to *answer every question*. Guess if you have to but include something for each question. Remember that you will receive no credit for a blank and will probably receive some credit if you write something in answer to an essay question. If you guess a letter – say "B" for a multiple-choice question – you may have guessed right. If you leave a blank as an answer to a multiple-choice question, the examiners may respect your feelings but it will not add a point to your score. Some exams may penalize you for wrong answers, so in such cases *only*, you may not want to guess unless you have some basis for your answer.

7) Suggestions
   a. Objective-type questions
      1. Examine the question booklet for proper sequence of pages and questions
      2. Read all instructions carefully
      3. Skip any question which seems too difficult; return to it after all other questions have been answered
      4. Apportion your time properly; do not spend too much time on any single question or group of questions
      5. Note and underline key words – *all, most, fewest, least, best, worst, same, opposite,* etc.
      6. Pay particular attention to negatives
      7. Note unusual option, e.g., unduly long, short, complex, different or similar in content to the body of the question
      8. Observe the use of "hedging" words – *probably, may, most likely,* etc.
      9. Make sure that your answer is put next to the same number as the question
      10. Do not second-guess unless you have good reason to believe the second answer is definitely more correct
      11. Cross out original answer if you decide another answer is more accurate; do not erase until you are ready to hand your paper in
      12. Answer all questions; guess unless instructed otherwise
      13. Leave time for review

   b. Essay questions
      1. Read each question carefully
      2. Determine exactly what is wanted. Underline key words or phrases.
      3. Decide on outline or paragraph answer

4. Include many different points and elements unless asked to develop any one or two points or elements
5. Show impartiality by giving pros and cons unless directed to select one side only
6. Make and write down any assumptions you find necessary to answer the questions
7. Watch your English, grammar, punctuation and choice of words
8. Time your answers; don't crowd material

8) Answering the essay question

Most essay questions can be answered by framing the specific response around several key words or ideas. Here are a few such key words or ideas:

M's: manpower, materials, methods, money, management
P's: purpose, program, policy, plan, procedure, practice, problems, pitfalls, personnel, public relations
   a. Six basic steps in handling problems:
      1. Preliminary plan and background development
      2. Collect information, data and facts
      3. Analyze and interpret information, data and facts
      4. Analyze and develop solutions as well as make recommendations
      5. Prepare report and sell recommendations
      6. Install recommendations and follow up effectiveness

   b. Pitfalls to avoid
      1. *Taking things for granted* – A statement of the situation does not necessarily imply that each of the elements is necessarily true; for example, a complaint may be invalid and biased so that all that can be taken for granted is that a complaint has been registered
      2. *Considering only one side of a situation* – Wherever possible, indicate several alternatives and then point out the reasons you selected the best one
      3. *Failing to indicate follow up* – Whenever your answer indicates action on your part, make certain that you will take proper follow-up action to see how successful your recommendations, procedures or actions turn out to be
      4. *Taking too long in answering any single question* – Remember to time your answers properly

IX. AFTER THE TEST

Scoring procedures differ in detail among civil service jurisdictions although the general principles are the same. Whether the papers are hand-scored or graded by machine we have described, they are nearly always graded by number. That is, the person who marks the paper knows only the number – never the name – of the applicant. Not until all the papers have been graded will they be matched with names. If other tests, such as training and experience or oral interview ratings have been given, scores will be combined. Different parts of the examination usually have different weights. For example, the written test might count 60 percent of the final grade, and a rating of training and experience 40 percent. In many jurisdictions, veterans will have a certain number of points added to their grades.

After the final grade has been determined, the names are placed in grade order and an eligible list is established. There are various methods for resolving ties between those who get the same final grade – probably the most common is to place first the name of the person whose application was received first. Job offers are made from the eligible list in the order the names appear on it. You will be notified of your grade and your rank as soon as all these computations have been made. This will be done as rapidly as possible.

People who are found to meet the requirements in the announcement are called "eligibles." Their names are put on a list of eligible candidates. An eligible's chances of getting a job depend on how high he stands on this list and how fast agencies are filling jobs from the list.

When a job is to be filled from a list of eligibles, the agency asks for the names of people on the list of eligibles for that job. When the civil service commission receives this request, it sends to the agency the names of the three people highest on this list. Or, if the job to be filled has specialized requirements, the office sends the agency the names of the top three persons who meet these requirements from the general list.

The appointing officer makes a choice from among the three people whose names were sent to him. If the selected person accepts the appointment, the names of the others are put back on the list to be considered for future openings.

That is the rule in hiring from all kinds of eligible lists, whether they are for typist, carpenter, chemist, or something else. For every vacancy, the appointing officer has his choice of any one of the top three eligibles on the list. This explains why the person whose name is on top of the list sometimes does not get an appointment when some of the persons lower on the list do. If the appointing officer chooses the second or third eligible, the No. 1 eligible does not get a job at once, but stays on the list until he is appointed or the list is terminated.

X. HOW TO PASS THE INTERVIEW TEST

The examination for which you applied requires an oral interview test. You have already taken the written test and you are now being called for the interview test – the final part of the formal examination.

You may think that it is not possible to prepare for an interview test and that there are no procedures to follow during an interview. Our purpose is to point out some things you can do in advance that will help you and some good rules to follow and pitfalls to avoid while you are being interviewed.

What is an interview supposed to test?
The written examination is designed to test the technical knowledge and competence of the candidate; the oral is designed to evaluate intangible qualities, not readily measured otherwise, and to establish a list showing the relative fitness of each candidate – as measured against his competitors – for the position sought. Scoring is not on the basis of "right" and "wrong," but on a sliding scale of values ranging from "not passable" to "outstanding." As a matter of fact, it is possible to achieve a relatively low score without a single "incorrect" answer because of evident weakness in the qualities being measured.

Occasionally, an examination may consist entirely of an oral test – either an individual or a group oral. In such cases, information is sought concerning the technical knowledges and abilities of the candidate, since there has been no written examination for this purpose. More commonly, however, an oral test is used to supplement a written examination.

Who conducts interviews?

The composition of oral boards varies among different jurisdictions. In nearly all, a representative of the personnel department serves as chairman. One of the members of the board may be a representative of the department in which the candidate would work. In some cases, "outside experts" are used, and, frequently, a businessman or some other representative of the general public is asked to serve. Labor and management or other special groups may be represented. The aim is to secure the services of experts in the appropriate field.

However the board is composed, it is a good idea (and not at all improper or unethical) to ascertain in advance of the interview who the members are and what groups they represent. When you are introduced to them, you will have some idea of their backgrounds and interests, and at least you will not stutter and stammer over their names.

What should be done before the interview?

While knowledge about the board members is useful and takes some of the surprise element out of the interview, there is other preparation which is more substantive. It *is* possible to prepare for an oral interview – in several ways:

1) Keep a copy of your application and review it carefully before the interview

This may be the only document before the oral board, and the starting point of the interview. Know what education and experience you have listed there, and the sequence and dates of all of it. Sometimes the board will ask you to review the highlights of your experience for them; you should not have to hem and haw doing it.

2) Study the class specification and the examination announcement

Usually, the oral board has one or both of these to guide them. The qualities, characteristics or knowledges required by the position sought are stated in these documents. They offer valuable clues as to the nature of the oral interview. For example, if the job involves supervisory responsibilities, the announcement will usually indicate that knowledge of modern supervisory methods and the qualifications of the candidate as a supervisor will be tested. If so, you can expect such questions, frequently in the form of a hypothetical situation which you are expected to solve. NEVER go into an oral without knowledge of the duties and responsibilities of the job you seek.

3) Think through each qualification required

Try to visualize the kind of questions you would ask if you were a board member. How well could you answer them? Try especially to appraise your own knowledge and background in each area, *measured against the job sought*, and identify any areas in which you are weak. Be critical and realistic – do not flatter yourself.

4) Do some general reading in areas in which you feel you may be weak

For example, if the job involves supervision and your past experience has NOT, some general reading in supervisory methods and practices, particularly in the field of human relations, might be useful. Do NOT study agency procedures or detailed manuals. The oral board will be testing your understanding and capacity, not your memory.

5) Get a good night's sleep and watch your general health and mental attitude

You will want a clear head at the interview. Take care of a cold or any other minor ailment, and of course, no hangovers.

What should be done on the day of the interview?

Now comes the day of the interview itself. Give yourself plenty of time to get there. Plan to arrive somewhat ahead of the scheduled time, particularly if your appointment is in the fore part of the day. If a previous candidate fails to appear, the board might be ready for you a bit early. By early afternoon an oral board is almost invariably behind schedule if there are many candidates, and you may have to wait. Take along a book or magazine to read, or your application to review, but leave any extraneous material in the waiting room when you go in for your interview. In any event, relax and compose yourself.

The matter of dress is important. The board is forming impressions about you – from your experience, your manners, your attitude, and your appearance. Give your personal appearance careful attention. Dress your best, but not your flashiest. Choose conservative, appropriate clothing, and be sure it is immaculate. This is a business interview, and your appearance should indicate that you regard it as such. Besides, being well groomed and properly dressed will help boost your confidence.

Sooner or later, someone will call your name and escort you into the interview room. *This is it.* From here on you are on your own. It is too late for any more preparation. But remember, you asked for this opportunity to prove your fitness, and you are here because your request was granted.

What happens when you go in?

The usual sequence of events will be as follows: The clerk (who is often the board stenographer) will introduce you to the chairman of the oral board, who will introduce you to the other members of the board. Acknowledge the introductions before you sit down. Do not be surprised if you find a microphone facing you or a stenotypist sitting by. Oral interviews are usually recorded in the event of an appeal or other review.

Usually the chairman of the board will open the interview by reviewing the highlights of your education and work experience from your application – primarily for the benefit of the other members of the board, as well as to get the material into the record. Do not interrupt or comment unless there is an error or significant misinterpretation; if that is the case, do not hesitate. But do not quibble about insignificant matters. Also, he will usually ask you some question about your education, experience or your present job – partly to get you to start talking and to establish the interviewing "rapport." He may start the actual questioning, or turn it over to one of the other members. Frequently, each member undertakes the questioning on a particular area, one in which he is perhaps most competent, so you can expect each member to participate in the examination. Because time is limited, you may also expect some rather abrupt switches in the direction the questioning takes, so do not be upset by it. Normally, a board member will not pursue a single line of questioning unless he discovers a particular strength or weakness.

After each member has participated, the chairman will usually ask whether any member has any further questions, then will ask you if you have anything you wish to add. Unless you are expecting this question, it may floor you. Worse, it may start you off on an extended, extemporaneous speech. The board is not usually seeking more information. The question is principally to offer you a last opportunity to present further qualifications or to indicate that you have nothing to add. So, if you feel that a significant qualification or characteristic has been overlooked, it is proper to point it out in a sentence or so. Do not compliment the board on the thoroughness of their examination – they have been sketchy, and you know it. If you wish, merely say, "No thank you, I have nothing further to add." This is a point where you can "talk yourself out" of a good impression or fail to present an important bit of information. Remember, *you close the interview yourself.*

The chairman will then say, "That is all, Mr. _____, thank you." Do not be startled; the interview is over, and quicker than you think. Thank him, gather your belongings and take your leave. Save your sigh of relief for the other side of the door.

How to put your best foot forward

Throughout this entire process, you may feel that the board individually and collectively is trying to pierce your defenses, seek out your hidden weaknesses and embarrass and confuse you. Actually, this is not true. They are obliged to make an appraisal of your qualifications for the job you are seeking, and they want to see you in your best light. Remember, they must interview all candidates and a non-cooperative candidate may become a failure in spite of their best efforts to bring out his qualifications. Here are 15 suggestions that will help you:

1) Be natural – Keep your attitude confident, not cocky

If you are not confident that you can do the job, do not expect the board to be. Do not apologize for your weaknesses, try to bring out your strong points. The board is interested in a positive, not negative, presentation. Cockiness will antagonize any board member and make him wonder if you are covering up a weakness by a false show of strength.

2) Get comfortable, but don't lounge or sprawl

Sit erectly but not stiffly. A careless posture may lead the board to conclude that you are careless in other things, or at least that you are not impressed by the importance of the occasion. Either conclusion is natural, even if incorrect. Do not fuss with your clothing, a pencil or an ashtray. Your hands may occasionally be useful to emphasize a point; do not let them become a point of distraction.

3) Do not wisecrack or make small talk

This is a serious situation, and your attitude should show that you consider it as such. Further, the time of the board is limited – they do not want to waste it, and neither should you.

4) Do not exaggerate your experience or abilities

In the first place, from information in the application or other interviews and sources, the board may know more about you than you think. Secondly, you probably will not get away with it. An experienced board is rather adept at spotting such a situation, so do not take the chance.

5) If you know a board member, do not make a point of it, yet do not hide it

Certainly you are not fooling him, and probably not the other members of the board. Do not try to take advantage of your acquaintanceship – it will probably do you little good.

6) Do not dominate the interview

Let the board do that. They will give you the clues – do not assume that you have to do all the talking. Realize that the board has a number of questions to ask you, and do not try to take up all the interview time by showing off your extensive knowledge of the answer to the first one.

7) Be attentive

You only have 20 minutes or so, and you should keep your attention at its sharpest throughout. When a member is addressing a problem or question to you, give him your undivided attention. Address your reply principally to him, but do not exclude the other board members.

8) Do not interrupt

A board member may be stating a problem for you to analyze. He will ask you a question when the time comes. Let him state the problem, and wait for the question.

9) Make sure you understand the question

Do not try to answer until you are sure what the question is. If it is not clear, restate it in your own words or ask the board member to clarify it for you. However, do not haggle about minor elements.

10) Reply promptly but not hastily

A common entry on oral board rating sheets is "candidate responded readily," or "candidate hesitated in replies." Respond as promptly and quickly as you can, but do not jump to a hasty, ill-considered answer.

11) Do not be peremptory in your answers

A brief answer is proper – but do not fire your answer back. That is a losing game from your point of view. The board member can probably ask questions much faster than you can answer them.

12) Do not try to create the answer you think the board member wants

He is interested in what kind of mind you have and how it works – not in playing games. Furthermore, he can usually spot this practice and will actually grade you down on it.

13) Do not switch sides in your reply merely to agree with a board member

Frequently, a member will take a contrary position merely to draw you out and to see if you are willing and able to defend your point of view. Do not start a debate, yet do not surrender a good position. If a position is worth taking, it is worth defending.

14) Do not be afraid to admit an error in judgment if you are shown to be wrong

The board knows that you are forced to reply without any opportunity for careful consideration. Your answer may be demonstrably wrong. If so, admit it and get on with the interview.

15) Do not dwell at length on your present job

The opening question may relate to your present assignment. Answer the question but do not go into an extended discussion. You are being examined for a *new* job, not your present one. As a matter of fact, try to phrase ALL your answers in terms of the job for which you are being examined.

Basis of Rating

Probably you will forget most of these "do's" and "don'ts" when you walk into the oral interview room. Even remembering them all will not ensure you a passing grade. Perhaps you did not have the qualifications in the first place. But remembering them will help you to put your best foot forward, without treading on the toes of the board members.

Rumor and popular opinion to the contrary notwithstanding, an oral board wants you to make the best appearance possible. They know you are under pressure – but they also want to see how you respond to it as a guide to what your reaction would be under the pressures of the job you seek. They will be influenced by the degree of poise you display, the personal traits you show and the manner in which you respond.

ABOUT THIS BOOK

This book contains tests divided into Examination Sections. Go through each test, answering every question in the margin. At the end of each test look at the answer key and check your answers. On the ones you got wrong, look at the right answer choice and learn. Do not fill in the answers first. Do not memorize the questions and answers, but understand the answer and principles involved. On your test, the questions will likely be different from the samples. Questions are changed and new ones added. If you understand these past questions you should have success with any changes that arise. Tests may consist of several types of questions. We have additional books on each subject should more study be advisable or necessary for you. Finally, the more you study, the better prepared you will be. This book is intended to be the last thing you study before you walk into the examination room. Prior study of relevant texts is also recommended. NLC publishes some of these in our Fundamental Series. Knowledge and good sense are important factors in passing your exam. Good luck also helps. So now study this Passbook, absorb the material contained within and take that knowledge into the examination. Then do your best to pass that exam.

EXAMINATION SECTION

EXAMINATION SECTION
TEST 1

DIRECTIONS: Each question or incomplete statement is followed by several suggested answers or completions. Select the one that BEST answers the question or completes the statement. *PRINT THE LETTER OF THE CORRECT ANSWER IN THE SPACE AT THE RIGHT.*

1. The temperature of the fuel oil leaving a preheater is controlled by a(n)   1._____

   A. potentiometer   B. relay
   C. low water cut-off   D. aquastat

2. A pneumatic tool is GENERALLY powered by   2._____

   A. natural gas   B. steam
   C. a battery   D. air

3. The maximum steam pressure permitted in the steam coils used for heating the coil in a submerged oil storage tank is MOST NEARLY _____ psi.   3._____

   A. 40   B. 35   C. 25   D. 10

4. The water pressure used in a hydrostatic test on a boiler is GENERALLY _____ the maximum working pressure.   4._____

   A. 4 times   B. 2 times
   C. 1 1/2 times   D. the same as

5. The one of the following valves that should be used in a steam line to throttle the flow is the _____ valve.   5._____

   A. plug   B. check   C. gate   D. globe

6. The CO (carbon monoxide) content in the flue gas from an efficiently fired boiler should be APPROXIMATELY _____ %.   6._____

   A. 0 to 1   B. 4 to 6   C. 8 to 10   D. 12 to 13

7. The CO_2 (carbon dioxide) percentage in the flue gas of an efficiently fired boiler should be APPROXIMATELY _____ %.   7._____

   A. 1   B. 12   C. 18   D. 25

8. When the temperature of stack gases rises considerably above the normal operating stack temperature, it GENERALLY indicates   8._____

   A. a low boiler water level
   B. a heavy smoke condition in the stack
   C. that the boiler is operating efficiently
   D. that the boiler tubes are dirty

9. The control which starts or stops the operation of the oil burner at a predetermined steam pressure is the   9._____

   A. pressuretrol   B. air flow interlock
   C. transformer   D. magnetic oil valve

1

10. In a closed feedwater heater, the water and the steam   10.___

    A. come into direct contact
    B. are kept apart from each other
    C. are under negative pressure
    D. mix and exhaust to the atmosphere

11. A *knocking* noise in steam lines is GENERALLY the result of   11.___

    A. superheated steam expansion
    B. high steam pressure
    C. condensation in the line
    D. rapid steam expansion

12. An electrical component known as a step-up transformer operates by raising   12.___

    A. voltage and decreasing amperage
    B. resistance and decreasing amperage
    C. amperage and decreasing resistance
    D. voltage and amperage at the same time

13. A manometer is an instrument that is used to measure   13.___

    A. heat radiation   B. air volume
    C. condensate water level   D. air pressure

14. Three 75-gallon per hour mechanical pressure type oil burners operating together are to   14.___
burn 150,000 gallons of No. 6 fuel oil.
The number of hours they would take to burn this amount of oil is MOST NEARLY

    A. 665   B. 760   C. 870   D. 1210

15. The sum of 10 1/2, 8 3/4, 5 1/2, and 2 1/4 is   15.___

    A. 23   B. 25   C. 26   D. 27

16. A water tank measures 50 feet long, 16 feet wide, and 12 feet high. Assume that water   16.___
weighs 60 pounds per cubic foot and that one gallon of water weighs 8 pounds.
The number of gallons the tank can hold when it is half full is

    A. 21,500   B. 28,375   C. 33,410   D. 36,000

17. Assuming 70 gallons of oil costs $42.00, then 110 gallons of oil at the same rate will cost   17.___

    A. $66   B. $84   C. $96   D. $152

18. The external heating area of a tube with an inside diarieter of 5", wall thickness of 1/4",   18.___
and length of 18' will be _____ sq.ft.

    A. 26   B. 28   C. 30   D. 32

19. The *burning* characteristic of coal MOST closely related to ash fusion temperatures is   19.___

    A. coking   B. bituminous
    C. lignite   D. sub-bituminous

20. What type of coal is used in the alternate method of stoking a hand-fired boiler?   20._____

    A. Anthracite   B. Bituminous
    C. Lignite   D. Sub-bituminous

Questions 21-25.

DIRECTIONS: Questions 21 through 25 are to be answered on the basis of the information
              contained in the following paragraph.

Fuel is conserved when a boiler is operating near its most efficient load. The efficiency of
a boiler will change as the output varies. Large amounts of air must be used at low ratings
and so the heat exchange is inefficient. As the output increases, the efficiency decreases due
to an increase in flue gas temperature. Every boiler has an output rate for which its efficiency
is highest. For example, in a water-tube boiler, the highest efficiency might occur at 120 percent of rated capacity, while in a vertical fire-tube boiler highest efficiency might be at 70% of
rated capacity. The type of fuel burned and cleanliness affect the maximum efficiency of the
boiler. When a power plant contains a battery of boilers, a sufficient number should be kept in
operation so as to maintain the output of individual units near their points of maximum efficiency. One of the boilers in the battery can be used as a regulator to meet the change in
demand for steam while the other boilers could still operate at their most efficient rating.
Boiler performance is expressed as the number of pounds of steam generated per pound of
fuel.

21. The number of pounds of steam generated per pound of fuel is a measure of boiler   21._____

    A. size   B. performance
    C. regulator input   D. bypass

22. The HIGHEST efficiency of a vertical fire-tube boiler might occur at _____% of _____   22._____
    capacity.

    A. 70; rated   B. 80; water tube
    C. 95; water tube   D. 120; rated

23. The MAXIMUM efficiency of a boiler is affected by   23._____

    A. atmospheric temperature   B. atmospheric pressure
    C. cleanliness   D. fire brick capacity

24. A heat exchanger uses large amounts of air at LOW   24._____

    A. fuel rates   B. ratings
    C. temperatures   D. pressures

25. One boiler in a battery of boilers should be used as a   25._____

    A. demand   B. standby   C. regulator   D. sneety

KEY (CORRECT ANSWERS)

1. D	11. C
2. D	12. A
3. D	13. D
4. C	14. A
5. D	15. D
6. A	16. D
7. B	17. A
8. D	18. A
9. A	19. A
10. B	20. A

21. B
22. A
23. C
24. B
25. C

TEST 2

DIRECTIONS: Each question or incomplete statement is followed by several suggested answers or completions. Select the one that BEST answers the question or completes the statement. *PRINT THE LETTER OF THE CORRECT ANSWER IN THE SPACE AT THE RIGHT.*

1. Mechanical atomizing oil burners in a completely automatic power boiler are lit by a(n)   1.____

    A. torch soaked with gasoline
    B. torch soaked with kerosene
    C. gas pilot flame
    D. electric spark

2. Which one of the following statements is MOST NEARLY correct ?   2.____

    A. The shape of the fire on a horizontal rotary burner can be controlled by the shape of the cup.
    B. The cup on a horizontal rotary cup burner rotates at 800 rpm.
    C. A horizontal rotary cup burner needs no blower.
    D. With a horizontal rotary cup burner, the oil does not need to be heated.

3. On a mechanical atomizing burner, the oil temperature should be MOST NEARLY _____ ° F.   3.____

    A. 84-140   B. 150-160   C. 182-225   D. 250-300

4. A fire breaks out in your oil storage room.
   After notifying the fire department, you should try to extinguish the fire by   4.____

    A. using a soda-acid extinguisher
    B. smothering the fire with a blanket
    C. using a stream of high-pressure water
    D. using a foamite portable extinguisher

5. What is the BIGGEST objection to the burning of bituminous coal?   5.____

    A. A large amount of air is required
    B. The coal will cake
    C. Grates are likely to be damaged
    D. Too much smoke

6. Hard scale is removed from the drum of a Stirling boiler by   6.____

    A. blowing down   B. pneumatic hamme
    C. high pressure air lance   D. steam lance

7. The BEST time to blow down a power boiler is   7.____

    A. after a low bank period
    B. at normal boiler rating
    C. at increased boiler rating
    D. after soot blowing

5

8. The slag screen in a water tube boiler would be the _____ row of tubes in the _____ bank.

   A. last; first
   C. first; third

   B. first; second
   D. first; first

   8.___

9. S.M.E. Code stipulates that at least one safety valve must be on a power boiler having a heating surface of less than _____ sq.ft.

   A. 2,000   B. 1,500   C. 1,000   D. 500

   9.___

10. The PROPER mixture of coal dust and air that should be maintained in a coal pulverizer is

   A. rich mixture
   B. lean mixture
   C. correct mixture to support combustion
   D. equal mixture of coal and air

   10.___

11. Plants operating in the city MOST likely would be burning coal with a moisture content of _____ %.

   A. 25   B. 15   C. 10   D. 5

   11.___

12. Eastern bituminous coal is graded in size, from largest to smallest, as follows:

   A. Run-of-mine, nut, lump
   B. Run-of-mine, nut, screenings
   C. Run-of-mine, lump, egg, nut, screenings
   D. Lump, egg, nut, stove, coal, slack

   12.___

13. A 35% volatile matter coal is

   A. lignite
   C. bituminous

   B. semi-bituminous
   D. anthracite

   13.___

14. A residual oil is

   A. light diesel oil
   C. bunker C

   B. kerosene
   D. #2 oil

   14.___

15. If an Orsat test shows O_2 above 8% in an oil fired boiler, what should be done?

   A. Clean dirty tubes
   B. Decrease air supply
   C. Lower fuel oil temperature
   D. Increase air supply

   15.___

16. On a mechanical atomizing oil burner, it is MOST NEARLY correct that

   A. fuel need not be heated
   B. capacity can be controlled by varying fuel pressure
   C. fuel feed is controlled by orifices
   D. burner parts need not be cleaned

   16.___

17. On a slow speed steam engine operating at 150 psi with atmosphere exhaust, the spring   17._____
    HOST likely to be used for an indicator is

    A. 40   B. 70   C. 100   D. 150

18. What is the APPROXIMATE horsepower of a double-acting 6" x 4" x 6" running at 400   18._____
    rpm with a steam pressure of 50 psig?

    A. 17   B. 24   C. 33   D. 45

19. The one of the following which may be used to heat feed water with boiler blowdown   19._____
    water in a continuous blowdown system is a(n)

    A. heat exchanger
    B. open feed water heater
    C. economizer
    D. deaerator feed water heater

20. A turbine generator at full load runs at 1,764 rpm. At no load, it runs at 1,800 rpm.   20._____
    Its speed regulation is MOST NEARLY _____%.

    A. 2   B. 4   C. 6   D. 8

21. A 4 pole motor operating on 60 cycles synchronous speed would have an rpm of   21._____

    A. 1800   B. 3600   C. 4600   D. 5600

22. On a DC compound wound motor, to change the rotation of the motor, you would change   22._____
    connections to the

    A. armature
    B. shunt field
    C. series field
    D. armature and series field

23. Modern boilers are generally constructed in such a manner that they are suspended   23._____
    from steel framework.
    This is NOT done to

    A. reduce stress on brickwork
    B. allow for thermal expansion
    C. eliminate the need for extensive foundations
    D. allow for increased heating surface

24. The term *wet boilers* may be used to describe a furnace in which   24._____

    A. coal which has been wetted in the bunker is burned
    B. the water walls extend to the bottom of the furnace
    C. the ash and slag collect at the furnace bottom in a molten pool
    D. a high fusion coal is burned

25. A water-lined fire box is constructed of

    A. a solid water box, used in place of refractory, into which feed water is fed
    B. water tubes in the fire box into which feed water is fed
    C. a series of water wall tubes around the fire box
    D. a cast iron water box in the front of the fire box

KEY (CORRECT ANSWERS)

1.	C		11.	D
2.	A		12.	D
3.	B		13.	A
4.	D		14.	C
5.	D		15.	B
6.	B		16.	B
7.	A		17.	D
8.	D		18.	A
9.	D		19.	A
10.	A		20.	A

21.	A
22.	A
23.	D
24.	C
25.	C

TEST 3

DIRECTIONS: Each question or incomplete statement is followed by several suggested answers or completions. Select the one that BEST answers the question or completes the statement. *PRINT THE LETTER OF THE CORRECT ANSWER IN THE SPACE AT THE RIGHT.*

1. A boiler safety valve is USUALLY set above the maximum working pressure by an amount equal to _____ % of the maximum working pressure.

    A. 6   B. 10   C. 12   D. 14

    1._____

2. The one of the following grades of fuel oil that contains the GREATEST heating value in BTU per gallon is #_____ oil.

    A. 2   B. 4   C. 5   D. 6

    2._____

3. To say that a fuel oil has a high *viscosity* is to mean that the fuel oil will

    A. evaporate easily
    B. burn without smoke
    C. flow slowly through pipes
    D. have a low specific gravity

    3._____

4. The bype of fuel oil pump GENERALLY used with a rotary cup oil burner system is the _____ pump.

    A. propeller   B. integral
    C. centrifugal   D. piston

    4._____

5. No. 6 fuel oil flowing to a mechanical atomizing burner should be preheated to APPROXIMATELY _____° F.

    A. 185   B. 115   C. 100   D. 80

    5._____

6. The flame of an industrial rotary cup oil burner should be adjusted so that the flame

    A. has a yellow color with blue spots
    B. strikes all sides of the combustion chamber
    C. has a light brown color
    D. does not strike the rear of the combustion chamber

    6._____

7. The location of the oil burner *remote control switch* should GENERALLY be

    A. at the boiler room entrance
    B. on the boiler shell
    C. on the oil burner motor
    D. on the wall nearest the boiler

    7._____

8. With forced draft, the approximate wind box pressure in a single-retort underfeed stoker is NORMALLY _____ inches.

    A. 2   B. 5   C. 7   D. 9

    8._____

9. The pressure over the fire in a coal-fired steam boiler with a balanced draft system and   9.___
   natural draft is MOST NEARLY _____ inches.

   A. +.60   B. +.50   C. -.02   D. -.70

10. Three tons of coal with an ash content of 10% will yield a weight of ash of MOST   10.___
    NEARLY _____ lbs.

    A. 400   B. 500   C. 600   D. 700

11. To clean and spread the coal over the grates of a coal-fired boiler, a stationary fireman   11.___
    would use a tool known as a (n)

    A. hoe   B. extractor   C. lance   D. slice bar

12. To burn the volatile matter in coal more efficiently, one should   12.___

    A. mix peat with the coal
    B. supply overfire draft
    C. mix it with a lower grade of coal
    D. add moisture to the coal

13. The one of the following that lists the size classifications of anthracite coal in proper   13.___
    order, ranging from the smallest to the largest, is

    A. chestnut, culm, pea, birdseye, egg
    B. egg, stove, pea, broken, culm
    C. stove, egg, birdseye, culm, broken
    D. birdseye, pea, chestnut, stove, egg

14. The fire in a hand-fired furnace can be cleaned by a method known as   14.___

    A. *ashpit to grate*   B. *bottom to top*
    C. *side to side*   D. *grate to crown*

15. Coal is normally *tempered* when operating a chain grate stoker for the purpose of   15.___

    A. increasing coking   B. preventing clinking
    C. collecting particles   D. promoting uniform burning

16. The CO_2 percentage in the flue gas of a power plant is indicated by a   16.___

    A. Doppler meter   B. Ranarex indicator
    C. microtector   D. hygrometer

17. The MOST likely cause of black smoke exhausting from the chimney of an oil-fired boiler   17.___
    is

    A. high secondary air flow   B. low stack emission
    C. low oil temperature   D. high chimney draft

18. The diameter of the steam piston in a steam-driven duplex vacuum pump whose dimen-   18.___
    sions are given as 3 x 2 x 4 is

    A. 2   B. 3   C. 4   D. 6

19. An induced draft fan is GENERALLY connected between the

   A. condenser and the first pass
   B. stack and the breeching
   C. feedwater heater and the boiler feed pump
   D. combustion chamber and fuel oil tanks

20. The purpose of an air chamber on a reciprocating water pump is to

   A. maintain a uniform flow
   B. reduce the amount of steam expansion
   C. create a pulsating flow
   D. vary the amount of steam admission

21. *Flash point* is the temperature at which oil will

   A. change completely to vapor
   B. safely fire in a furnace
   C. flash into flame if a lighted match is passed just above the top of the oil
   D. burn intermittently when ignited

22. A *sounding box* would NORMALLY be found

   A. on top of the boiler
   B. next to a compressed air tank
   C. in a fuel oil tank
   D. in a steam condenser

23. An *intercooler* is GENERALLY found on a(n)

   A. steam pump   B. air compressor
   C. steam engine   D. rotary oil pump

24. The instrument used to measure atmospheric pressure is a

   A. capillary tube   B. venturi
   C. barometer   D. calorimeter

25. The bottom blowdown on a boiler is used to

   A. remove mud drum water impurities
   B. increase boiler priming
   C. reduce steam pressure in the header
   D. increase the boiler water level

KEY (CORRECT ANSWERS)

1.	A		11.	A
2.	D		12.	B
3.	C		13.	D
4.	C		14.	C
5.	B		15.	D
6.	D		16.	B
7.	A		17.	C
8.	A		18.	A
9.	C		19.	B
10.	C		20.	A

21.	B
22.	C
23.	B
24.	C
25.	A

——————

EXAMINATION SECTION
TEST 1

DIRECTIONS: Each question or incomplete statement is followed by several suggested answers or completions Select the one that BEST answers the question or completes the statement. *PRINT THE LETTER OF THE CORRECT ANSWER IN THE SPACE AT THE RIGHT.*

1. Of the following types of boilers, the one which is MOST likely to have drilled staybolts is   1.____

    A. Stirling
    B. sectional or serpentine header straight water tube
    C. box header straight water tube
    D. D frame water tube complete with water wall

2. If you looked in the furnace and saw a very white fire, it would indicate   2.____

    A. excess air   B. not enough air
    C. a thin fuel bed   D. clinkers

3. The CO_2 in the flue gases is 14% over the fire, 11% in the second pass, 8% at the damper.   3.____
    This MOST likely indicates

    A. leaks through side walls
    B. not enough air under the fire
    C. too much air under the fire
    D. incomplete combustion

4. When the #5 Ringelmann chart matches the smoke coming from the top of a stack, the indication is   4.____

    A. excess air
    B. not enough air
    C. stoker operating too fast
    D. stoker operating too slow

5. A hand-fired coal burning boiler furnace is equipped with forced draft. In its operation, it is noted that the fires are bright and smokeless and that CO_2 is 7.5%. Under these conditions, the probability is that   5.____

    A. there is excess air
    B. there is nothing wrong with the way the boiler furnace is being operated
    C. there is too little air to obtain complete combustion
    D. a barometric damper should be installed

6. When firing bituminous coal by hand, GENERALLY you should fire   6.____

    A. periodically and heavy   B. frequently and lightly
    C. frequently and heavily   D. the high spots

7. What type of coal is used in the *alternate* method of stoking a hand-fired boiler?   7.____

    A. Anthracite   B. Bituminous
    C. Lignite   D. Semi-bituminous

8. The *even spread method* is used in firing _____ fuel.   8.__

   A. bituminous   B. anthracite
   C. lignite   D. semi-bituminous

9. The MAXIMUM allowable pressure, in lbs. per sq.in., for a fusible plug is   9.__

   A. 100   B. 150   C. 200   D. 250

10. The fusible plug on a vertical fire tube boiler USUALLY is located   10.__

    A. next to the safety valve
    B. next to the steam gauge
    C. in the lowest tube sheet
    D. in the outside tube

11. Where is a forced draft fan connected?   11.__

    A. At the stack
    B. At the last pass of a boiler
    C. Between the atmosphere and the fuel burning equipment
    D. In the furnace

12. The MOST efficient method of regulating the capacity of a forced draft fan installed on a   12.__
    boiler is to

    A. control the inlet damper
    B. regulate fan speed
    C. regulate fan discharge damper
    D. cut the fan in and out

13. Forced draft and induced draft fans in modern steam plants are driven by a(n)   13.__

    A. steam turbine   B. series motor
    C. AC motor   D. steam engine

14. When natural draft is used with stokers, the ash pit must be sealed so that no loss of air   14.__
    will result.
    This sealed ash pit is referred to as a

    A. natural draft wind box   B. atmospheric wind box
    C. *coke dam*   D. barometric wind box

15. The boiler that has the fusible plug in the crown sheet is the _____ boiler.   15.__

    A. H.R.T.   B. locomotive
    C. water-tube   D. A type or A frame Navy

16. An Ogee ring would be found on a _____ boiler.   16.__

    A. Scotch   B. Stirling
    C. bent-tube   D. dry-top vertical (Manning)

17. A certain boiler contains one tube thicker than the rest, in which the fusible plug is installed.
Of the following, the boiler type BEST fitting the above description is the

    A. H.R.T.
    B. vertical fire-tube *dry-top* with exposed tubes
    C. vertical fire-tube *wet-top* with submerged tubes
    D. Scotch marine

17.____

18. Scale forms from boiler water deposits on the outside of the tubes of _____ boilers.

    A. longitudinal-drum water-tube
    B. cross-drum water-tube
    C. horizontal return tubular
    D. Stirling

18.____

19. An inside fusible plug will melt when its temperature reaches _____ °F.

    A. 200-300   B. 300-400   C. 400-500   D. 500-600

19.____

20. Of the following types of boilers, the one in which you would find staybolts is the

    A. Stirling
    B. vertical water-tube
    C. longitudinal drum with box headers
    D. water-tube with serpentine or sinuous headers

20.____

21. If you were firing a steam-size anthracite coal boiler by hand, what would be the percent of ash you would expect to find when cleaning, assuming that the grates and furnace were in good condition and that proper combustion was obtained?

    A. 40%   B. 5%   C. 25%   D. 15%

21.____

22. If a coal tested has an ash fusion temperature of 2500 °F, slag would start to form on the boiler tubes at _____ °F.

    A. 2600   B. 2400   C. 2450   D. 2700

22.____

23. In hand firing a boiler, air is admitted over the fire to

    A. cut smoke   B. cool the furnace
    C. cool the grates   D. prevent a blow-back

23.____

24. In a well-designed, well-operated, hand-fired boiler, the GREATEST heat loss comes from

    A. radiation   B. thick fuel bed
    C. excess air   D. draft too high

24.____

25. The furnace of a coal-fired steam boiler is USUALLY _____ °F.

    A. 1500   B. 2500   C. 3500   D. 4500

25.____

KEY (CORRECT ANSWERS)

1.	D	11.	C
2.	A	12.	B
3.	A	13.	C
4.	B	14.	B
5.	A	15.	B
6.	B	16.	D
7.	A	17.	B
8.	B	18.	C
9.	C	19.	C
10.	D	20.	B

21.	D
22.	D
23.	A
24.	C
25.	B

TEST 2

DIRECTIONS: Each question or incomplete statement is followed by several suggested answers or completions. Select the one that BEST answers the question or completes the statement. *PRINT THE LETTER OF THE CORRECT ANSWER IN THE SPACE AT THE RIGHT.*

1. The maintenance cost of an underfeed stoker, compared to that of an overfeed stoker, is   1.____

    A. slightly less
    B. somewhat higher
    C. practically the same
    D. considerably less

2. The fuel bed depth of an underfeed stoker operating under normal conditions is MOST NEARLY _____".   2.____

    A. 4 to 8
    B. 10 to 24
    C. 20 to 30
    D. 30 to 40

3. The purpose of an arch on a stoker-fired boiler is to   3.____

    A. regulate the coal feed
    B. make the draft greater
    C. help burn volatile content in fuel by heating the green coal
    D. help level the fuel bed

4. In the city, the sludge and mud from the mud drum are USUALLY blown   4.____

    A. into a tank and, after a cooling down period, drained into the city sewer
    B. into a tank wagon and carted away
    C. directly into the city sewer
    D. pumped by means of a centrifugal pump into the city sewer

5. A syphon breaker on a blowdown tank is connected to the sewer line and the   5.____

    A. cold water inlet
    B. cold water outlet
    C. blowdown line
    D. vent

6. When preparing a boiler for a hydrostatic test, the CORRECT procedure is to   6.____

    A. dump fires, clean grates, ash pit, tubes, and breaching, and open manholes and handholes
    B. dump fires, clean grates, ash pit, tubes, and breaching, and fill boiler with water up to gagged safety valves
    C. run plant as usual
    D. wait for inspector to give directions

7. A cycling clock is used to   7.____

    A. indicate a smoking condition
    B. operate sprinklers to quench fire
    C. control operation of incinerator equipment
    D. operate hopper doors

8. Overfire air is brought into the furnace through   8.____

    A. the charging flue
    B. the ash pit door
    C. the purge damper
    D. an overfire air manifold

9. Underfire air, which passes through the grates and refuse, should be _____% of the total air required.

    A. 25   B. 50   C. 75   D. 100

9.___

10. Overfire air is introduced into the furnace for the purpose of

    A. cooling the furnace
    B. complete combustion and turbulence
    C. diluting the smoke
    D. agitating the ash

10.___

11. A purge damper is located

    A. above the highest hopper door
    B. under the grate
    C. in the bypass flue
    D. in the separation chamber

11.___

12. Boilers, drums, etc. sometimes develop cracks.
When repairing these cracks with *hard patches*, _____ is(are) used to repair the crack with the patch plate.

    A. bolts   B. weld
    C. rivets   D. stay bolt and weld

12.___

13. If there is no water in the gauge glass and no water comes from the lower try cock, you should

    A. close the steam outlet valve
    B. increase the supply of feed water
    C. open the safety valve
    D. stop the supply of coal and air

13.___

14. If a tube bursts, you should

    A. close the steam outlet valve
    B. close the feed water valve
    C. increase the speed of the stoker
    D. close the outlet damper

14.___

15. One MAJOR advantage of pulverized coal is

    A. little equipment is required
    B. the flue is comparatively clean
    C. slagging in the furnace is reduced
    D. a low amount of excess air can be used

15.___

16. One of the GREATEST difficulties in the satisfactory burning of pulverized coal has resulted from the

    A. lack of proper metals
    B. design of furnaces
    C. formation of slag
    D. method used for pulverizing the fuel

16.___

17. When you open the stack damper, the fire 17.____

    A. smokes   B. burns faster
    C. burns slower   D. none of the above

18. The Boiler Code permits the use of _____ safety valves. 18.____

    A. dead weight   B. weighted lever
    C. spring loaded   D. all of the above

19. The *blowdown* or *blowback* of a new type safety valve can be INCREASED by 19.____

    A. increasing the tension of the main spring
    B. decreasing the tension of the main spring
    C. raising the blowdown adjusting ring
    D. lowering the blowdown adjusting ring

Questions 20-21.

DIRECTIONS: Questions 20 and 21 are to be answered on the basis of the following information.

    All large power boilers are provided with a water column upon which the water-gauge
glass, gauge-cocks, and steam gauge are mounted.

20. The MINIMUM permitted size of water column pipe connections to the boiler is _____ 20.____
    inch.

    A. 1/2   B. 3/4   C. 1   D. 1 1/4

21. The MINIMUM permitted size of water column pipe connections to the drain is _____ 21.____
    inch.

    A. 1/2   B. 3/4   C. 1   D. 1 1/4

22. Every power boiler must be provided with at least one water-gauge glass which may be 22.____
connected directly to the boiler or to an intervening water column.
The vertical distance between the minimum permissible water level in the boiler and
the lowest visible portion of the glass must be AT LEAST _____ inch(es).

    A. 6   B. 4   C. 2   D. 1

23. Every power boiler must also be provided with gauge cocks or try cocks located within 23.____
the visible length of the water-gauge glass, unless two independently connected water-
gauge glasses are provided.
The MINIMUM number of gauge-cocks required is

    A. 1   B. 2   C. 3   D. 4

24. Boiler feed water is being fed into the boiler. On each stroke of the pump, there is a heavy 24.____
pound in the line. The MOST reasonable cause of this pound is the

    A. air chamber on the pump is too small
    B. pump is working too fast
    C. check valve is binding
    D. piston is loose on the piston rod

25. Tuyeres are used to

    A. maintain an even fuel bed
    B. furnish air for coal
    C. assist in ash removal
    D. spread coal across the stoker

25.___

_____

KEY (CORRECT ANSWERS)

1.	B		11.	A
2.	B		12.	C
3.	C		13.	D
4.	A		14.	A
5.	D		15.	D
6.	B		16.	C
7.	C		17.	B
8.	D		18.	C
9.	C		19.	D
10.	B		20.	C

21.	B
22.	C
23.	C
24.	A
25.	B

_____

TEST 3

DIRECTIONS: Each question or incomplete statement is followed by several suggested answers or completions. Select the one that BEST answers the question or completes the statement. *PRINT THE LETTER OF THE CORRECT ANSWER IN THE SPACE AT THE RIGHT.*

1. The grate surface of a stoker-fed boiler, in comparison to a hand-fired boiler of equal steaming capacity, is   1._____

   A. greater
   B. less
   C. equal
   D. stoker boilers don't have grates

2. With an overfeed stoker, the grate surface merely carries the fuel through the furnace to the point where the ash is dumped into the ash pit.   2._____
   Therefore, coal used in this type of stoker having high ash content

   A. has a tendency to have an abrasive effect on the stoker parts
   B. protects the grate surface from radiation
   C. increases the loss of combustibles in the ash pit
   D. has a tendency to form large clinkers

3. The coal feed to a fire flows upward and over the grate in a(n) _____ stoker.   3._____

   A. underfeed   B. overfeed
   C. spreader   D. chain grate

4. What will happen if a boiler is provided with dump grates and the operator does NOT dump the ash at regular intervals?   4._____

   A. Increased fuel combustion
   B. Decreased fuel combustion
   C. Excessive flue ash
   D. Burned grates

5. A throttling calorimeter is used for testing the   5._____

   A. quality of coal   B. density of smoke
   C. quality of steam   D. quantity of steam

6. Blowdown water in large plants is sometimes used for   6._____

   A. heating feed water   B. make-up water
   C. wetting down coal   D. condensing purposes

7. The Boiler Code of the _____ regulates boilers inspected in the City of New York.   7._____

   A. U.S. Bureau of Standards
   B. N.Y.C. Board of Standards and Appeals
   C. Middle Atlantic States Boiler Inspectors' Conference
   D. New York State Department of Labor

8. A steam jet installed on a boiler can be used for   8.___

    A. draft   B. cleaning
    C. drying   D. steaming out

9. To check an F-12 system for leaks, you would use a(n)   9.___

    A. candle   B. halide torch
    C. punk stick   D. litmus paper

10. An optical pyrometer is an instrument used to determine   10.___

    A. stack temperature   B. furnace temperature
    C. draft pressure   D. furnace pressure

11. While on watch, if the safety valve sticks open on an operating boiler, you should   11.___

    A. secure the boiler
    B. let the pressure rise
    C. let the pressure drop to reseating pressure and use the hand lifting gear
    D. tap the valve with a sledge

12. Which of the following is NOT a good method of preventing spontaneous combustion of   12.___
    bituminous coal piled in storage?

    A. Circulate air through the pile
    B. Keep the coal wet
    C. Cover the pile with a tarpaulin
    D. Spread tar or asphalt over the pile to keep out the air

13. A boiler making steam at 200 pounds per square inch pressure uses coal.   13.___
    Which coal will have the HIGHEST BTU content?

    A. Anthracite   B. High volatile bituminous
    C. Semi-bituminous   D. Lignite

14. GENERALLY, anthracite has _____ BTU than _____.   14.___

    A. more; bituminous   B. less; lignite
    C. less; sub-bituminous   D. less; bituminous

15. The heating value of a certain fuel is given as 18,000 BTU per pound.   15.___
    What kind of fuel is it?

    A. Anthracite coal   B. Bituminous coal
    C. Fuel oil   D. Wood

16. The heating value of No. 6 fuel oil, in BTU per gallon, is APPROXIMATELY   16.___

    A. 142,500 to 144,500   B. 148,500 to 150,500
    C. 154,500 to 156,500   D. 160,500 to 162,500

17. Anthracite coal has   17.___

    A. high ash content, low BTU value
    B. low ash content, high BUT value
    C. more volatile matter than bituminous
    D. less volatile matter than bituminous

18. A proximate analysis shows a fuel to have 4% volatile matter. **18.____**
What kind of fuel is it?

   A. Anthracite   B. Semi-bituminous
   C. Bituminous   D. Lignite

19. Anthracite coal _____ than bituminous coal. **19.____**

   A. has more volatile matter
   B. has more ash
   C. is easier to grind in a pulverizer
   D. has a higher heating value

20. If a boiler is provided with clinker grinder rolls and the pit is allowed to fill up to the point **20.____**
where it prevents the coal from moving down the retorts,

   A. the tuyeres will burn up
   B. clinkers will form
   C. the stoker will stall due to overload
   D. the shearing pin on the stoker will break

21. Comparing a hand-fired and a stoker-fired boiler, a stoker-fired boiler would **21.____**

   A. be less efficient
   B. be more efficient
   C. require less maintenance
   D. obtain greater steam pressure

22. Where will you find a shear pin? **22.____**

   A. Stoker   B. Engine
   C. Turbine   D. Air compressor

23. On what type of stoker would you be MOST likely to find a shear pin? **23.____**

   A. Spreader   B. Chain grate
   C. Underfeed   D. Overfeed

24. If you had tramp iron in an underfeed stoker, it would **24.____**

   A. decrease combustion   B. burn in the hot fire
   C. cause shear pin failure   D. cause an alarm to ring

25. A _____ stoker is used for caking bituminous coal. **25.____**

   A. travelling grate   B. chain grate
   C. spreader   D. multiple retort underfeed

KEY (CORRECT ANSWERS)

1.	B		11.	C
2.	B		12.	A
3.	A		13.	C
4.	B		14.	D
5.	C		15.	C
6.	A		16.	B
7.	D		17.	D
8.	A		18.	A
9.	B		19.	B
10.	B		20.	D

21.	B
22.	A
23.	C
24.	C
25.	D

———

EXAMINATION SECTION
TEST 1

DIRECTIONS: Each question or incomplete statement is followed by several suggested answers or completions. Select the one that BEST answers the question or completes the statement. *PRINT THE LETTER OF THE CORRECT ANSWER IN THE SPACE AT THE RIGHT.*

1. An *unloader* is a device that is commonly found on a(n)

    A. steam header   B. air compressor
    C. anemometer   D. soot blower

1._____

2. An instrument for drawing a diagram showing actual pressure-volume relationships within the cylinder of an engine or a compressor is called a(n)

    A. barometer   B. engine indicator
    C. pyrometer   D. venturi meter

2._____

3. Air compressor suction and discharge valves should be cleaned with

    A. naphtha   B. benzene   C. fuel oil   D. soap suds

3._____

4. Of the following valves, the BEST one to use to restrict or throttle a flow of fluid is a _____ valve.

    A. gate   B. quick-opening
    C. globe   D. plug

4._____

5. The MAIN reason that try-cocks are installed on a boiler is to ensure that the

    A. boiler can be blown down
    B. water column can be blown down
    C. water gage glass is operating correctly
    D. condensate pumps are operating

5._____

6. A direct-acting duplex reciprocating steam pump is designated as 6 x 3 x 7. The numeral 6 indicates the

    A. diameter of the water cylinders
    B. length of stroke of both cylinders
    C. diameter of the steam cylinders
    D. diameter of the admission valve

6._____

7. The one of the following pumps that has NO moving parts is the _____ pump.

    A. plunger   B. jet
    C. radial flow   D. piston

7._____

8. Of the following types of pumps, the one which is MOST generally used to pump fuel oil is the _____ type pump.

    A. jet   B. rotary
    C. centrifugal   D. propeller

8._____

9. The test pressure recommended for a hydrostatic test of a boiler is _____ the working pressure. 9.__

   A. 2 1/2 times   B. 2 times   C. 1 1/2 times   D. equal to

10. Assume that a boiler has been out of service for repairs and is now ready to be put back on the line. 10.__
    Of the following, the FIRST step operating personnel should take is to

    A. fill the boiler with water
    B. open the vents
    C. blow boiler tubes
    D. inspect the inside and outside of the boiler

11. The one of the following that is a water-tube boiler is the _____ boiler. 11.__

    A. horizontal return tubular
    B. bent-tube
    C. economic
    D. horizontal two-pass

12. An oil-fired high pressure boiler has to be taken off the line. 12.__
    Of the following procedures, the FIRST step would be to

    A. reduce the fuel feed and slowly decrease the output
    B. manually close the non-return valve
    C. open the drain connections between the non-return and the head stop valve
    D. close the feedwater-supply valve

13. A drop in steam pressure, as indicated by the steam gauge, of a normally operating steam boiler would MOST likely indicate that the 13.__

    A. fuel supply must be increased
    B. boiler must be blown down
    C. speed of the feedwater pump must be increased
    D. low water cut-off is inoperative

14. Steam that has been heated above the temperature corresponding to its pressure is said to be 14.__

    A. superheated   B. pressurized
    C. tempered   D. overheated

15. In a shutdown of a boiler to prevent the creation of a vacuum from the condensing steam within the boiler, the steam drum vent valve should be opened when the steam pressure has dropped to approximately _____ psi. 15.__

    A. 100   B. 75   C. 50   D. 25

16. An attemperator is a device used to control or regulate 16.__

    A. air temperature   B. steam temperature
    C. oil pressure   D. water pressure

17. The number of safety valves on the boiler drum of a power boiler with a heating surface of 500 square feet is AT LEAST   17.____

   A. 2   B. 3   C. 4   D. 5

18. The fusible plug of an HRT boiler is located in the   18.____

   A. hot water tank   B. rear head
   C. fire door   D. water column

19. Boiler tube size is designated by its   19.____

   A. boiler location   B. wall thickness
   C. external diameter   D. internal diameter

20. A feedwater heater is installed in a steam generating system PRIMARILY to   20.____

   A. furnish hot water to the building
   B. generate hot feedwater for the building radiators
   C. condition and heat feedwater to the boiler
   D. distribute high pressure steam

KEY (CORRECT ANSWERS)

1.	B		11.	B
2.	B		12.	A
3.	D		13.	A
4.	C		14.	A
5.	C		15.	D
6.	C		16.	B
7.	B		17.	A
8.	B		18.	B
9.	C		19.	C
10.	D		20.	C

TEST 2

Each question or incomplete statement is followed by several suggested answers or completions. Select the one that BEST answers the question or completes the statement. *PRINT THE LETTER OF THE CORRECT ANSWER IN THE SPACE AT THE RIGHT.*

1. A balanced draft in a boiler consists of   1.__

    A. a forced draft fan only
    B. a natural chimney draft only
    C. both forced and induced draft
    D. both induced and natural draft

2. One horsepower is *electrically equivalent* to 746   2.__

    A. watts   B. calories   C. joules   D. kilowatts

3. Of the following pH values, the one which indicates that a solution is *neither* acid *nor* alkaline is   3.__

    A. 3   B. 4   C. 7   D. 10

4. Zinc bars are sometimes placed in boilers to   4.__

    A. increase the pH value of the feedwater
    B. eliminate foul gases in the steam
    C. prevent corrosion
    D. decrease foaming and priming

5. The MAIN function of an evaporator is to remove impurities in   5.__

    A. air   B. oil   C. water   D. grease

6. The MAIN reason why a caustic boil-out of a boiler would be necessary is that the boiler has accumulated a deposit of   6.__

    A. sediment   B. oil   C. scale   D. slime

7. Of the following, the type of steam traps that does NOT have any moving parts is the   7.__

    A. inverted bucket   B. impulse
    C. continuous-flow   D. float-actuated

8. The one of the following valves that permits fluid to flow in one direction only is the   8.__

    A. check   B. plug   C. globe   D. stop

9. A 1/2 inch diameter galvanized pipe that is 3" long and has male threads at both ends is known as a   9.__

    A. tube   B. flange   C. joint   D. nipple

10. The one of the following pipe fittings that should be used to connect a 1 1/2"-diameter pipe is a(n)   10.__

    A. saddle   B. increaser   C. elbow   D. nipple

11. A receiver in a compressed air system 11.____

    A. stores lubricating oil
    B. stores compressed air
    C. furnishes air to the air compressor
    D. acts as a pressure relief

12. The device that stops or starts a fully automatic oil burner at a predetermined pressure is 12.____
called a

    A. hydrostat   B. thermostat
    C. pressuretrol   D. transformer

13. Of the following statements, the one which is CORRECT as pertains to a closed-type 13.____
feedwater heater is that the

    A. steam and water mix
    B. water will be heated to within a few degrees of the steam temperature
    C. feedwater heater is located at an elevation above the boiler feed pump
    D. floating impurities are removed from the surface of the water through the overflow
        weir

14. The function of *cooling towers* is to 14.____

    A. cool condenser water
    B. supply drinking water
    C. cool the boiler room
    D. circulate the boiler feedwater

15. The function of an oil separator in a non-condensing steam plant is to remove oil from 15.____

    A. exhaust steam   B. compressed air
    C. feedwater   D. liquid ammonia

16. An economizer is generally located between the 16.____

    A. feedwater heater and feed pump
    B. air compressor and receiver
    C. suction and discharge oil strainers
    D. boiler and the stack

17. Of the following types of equipment used to remove fly ash from flue gases, the one 17.____
which is the MOST commonly installed in commercial boilers is the

    A. electrostatic precipitator
    B. mechanical collector
    C. fabric filter
    D. wet scrubber

18. The one of the following general classes of stokers in which coal is admitted below the 18.____
point of air admission is the _____ stoker.

    A. underfeed   B. chain grate
    C. traveling grate   D. spreader

19. The fuel bed of an underfeed stoker has the green coal at the

19.__

    A. bottom   B. top
    C. middle   D. burning surface

20. The one of the following coals that has a restriction on its use in New York City is

20.__

    A. canel   B. lignite
    C. bituminous   D. anthracite

KEY (CORRECT ANSWERS)

1.	C	11.	B
2.	A	12.	C
3.	C	13.	B
4.	C	14.	A
5.	C	15.	A
6.	B	16.	D
7.	C	17.	A
8.	A	18.	A
9.	D	19.	A
10.	B	20.	C

EXAMINATION SECTION
TEST 1

DIRECTIONS: Each question or incomplete statement is followed by several suggested answers or completions. Select the one that BEST answers the question or completes the statement. *PRINT THE LETTER OF THE CORRECT ANSWER IN THE SPACE AT THE RIGHT.*

1. The method used in a hand-fired furnace wherein the coal is fired on one side of the furnace while the other side is burning brightly is known as the _____ method.

    A. coking   B. spreading   C. ribbon   D. alternate

1._____

2. The measure of a fluid's resistance to flow is known as

    A. viscosity   B. hydrodynamics
    C. continuity   D. polarity

2._____

3. Demulsibility is the ability of a lubricating oil to separate from

    A. air   B. steam   C. flue gas   D. water

3._____

4. The wick in a gravity oil-feed system is generally made of

    A. rayon   B. wool   C. cotton   D. nylon

4._____

5. The temperature range to which No. 6 low sulphur fuel oil must *normally* be heated for proper atomization is _____ °F.

    A. 220-240   B. 170-200   C. 140-160   D. 120-130

5._____

6. When fuel oil is dispersed from an oil burner as a fine mist, it is said to be

    A. impelled   B. atomized
    C. crystallized   D. filtered

6._____

7. The one of the following devices that controls the fuel oil temperature leaving the oil heater is a (n)

    A. interlock   B. aquastat
    C. modutrol   D. accumulator

7._____

8. A duplex oil strainer is installed in a fuel oil line to

    A. remove impurities at twice the rate of oil flow
    B. change the direction of flow of the oil
    C. facilitate the use of various grades of oil
    D. allow uninterrupted flow of oil when one strainer is removed and cleaned

8._____

9. The oil burner *remote control switch* should generally be located

    A. on the oil burner housing
    B. at the entrance to the boiler room
    C. on a wall nearest the oil transfer pump
    D. on top of the boiler drum

9._____

10. The control that starts and stops the flow of oil to the spinning cup of a rotary cup oil burner is the   10.___

    A. magnetic oil valve   B. transformer
    C. electrode   D. bellows

11. Spontaneous combustion ignition is MOST likely to occur in a pile of   11.___

    A. loose planks   B. oily tools
    C. oily rags   D. masonite scrapings

12. Electric current is measured in units of   12.___

    A. ohms   B. amperes   C. volts   D. farads

13. A circuit breaker serves the same function as a   13.___

    A. meter   B. resistor   C. fuse   D. solenoid

14. A lead expansion anchor would normally be used to attach a bracket to a   14.___

    A. plaster ceiling   B. masonite wall
    C. brass pipe   D. concrete wall

15. The hardness of water is expressed in units of   15.___

    A. gpm   B. ppm   C. cop   D. stp

16. The alkaline contents of boiler feedwater can be *decreased* by   16.___

    A. blowing down the boiler
    B. adding caustic soda
    C. increasing the firing rate
    D. decreasing the speed of the feedwater pump

17. The MAJOR cause of air pollution resulting from burning fuel oil is   17.___

    A. carbon monoxide   B. sulphur dioxide
    C. nitrogen   D. hydrogen

18. The CO_2 content in the flue gas of an efficiently fired boiler should be approximately   18.___

    A. 30%   B. 25%   C. 15%   D. 12%

19. Of the following devices, the one which is used to determine the CO_2 content in flue gases is a(n)   19.___

    A. orsat   B. haze gauge
    C. ammeter   D. venturi

20. The one of the following that is known as an *actuating control* is a   20.___

    A. bellows   B. heliostat
    C. needle valve   D. relay

KEY (CORRECT ANSWERS)

1.	D	11.	C
2.	A	12.	B
3.	D	13.	C
4.	B	14.	D
5.	B	15.	B
6.	B	16.	A
7.	B	17.	B
8.	D	18.	D
9.	B	19.	A
10.	A	20.	D

TEST 2

Each question or incomplete statement is followed by several suggested answers or completions. Select the one that BEST answers the question or completes the statement. *PRINT THE LETTER OF THE CORRECT ANSWER IN THE SPACE AT THE RIGHT.*

1. The function of a *pyrometer* is to measure   1.___

   A. hardness   B. vibration
   C. polarity   D. temperature

2. A simplex type Bourdon-tube gauge is *ordinarily* used on a steam boiler to indicate   2.___

   A. height   B. flow
   C. temperature   D. pressure

3. A *hydrometer* will measure   3.___

   A. specific weight   B. viscosity
   C. specific gravity   D. water level

4. An instrument that is used to measure gas pressure is a   4.___

   A. tachometer   B. spectrometer
   C. potentiometer   D. manometer

5. The packing that is *generally* used on the cold water end of a centrifugal pump is   5.___

   A. brass   B. rubber
   C. flax   D. graphited-asbestos

6. The one of the following wrenches that would *normally* be used on hexagonally-shaped   6.___
   screwed valves and fittings is the _____ wrench.

   A. open-end   B. torque
   C. adjustable pipe   D. hook spanner

7. A *hickey* is a device that is used to   7.___

   A. hang pipe
   B. lift heavy fittings
   C. dig a trench for a steam line
   D. bend pipe

8. A pneumatic tool is *normally* operated by   8.___

   A. propane   B. water   C. steam   D. air

9. If 50 gallons of fuel oil cost $30.00, then 60 gallons of oil at the same rate will cost   9.___

   A. $125.00   B. $90.00   C. $36.00   D. $25.00

10. Four oil burners using 50 gallons per hour operating together are to burn 100,000 gallons   10.___
    of No. 6 fuel oil. The number of hours that it would take to burn this quantity of oil is

    A. 500   B. 650   C. 825   D. 1,000

11. The floor area of a boiler room that is 52 feet long and 31 feet wide is _____ square feet.   11.____

   A. 1,562   B. 1,612   C. 1,721   D. 1,832

12. The sum of 5 1/2, 4, 3 1/4, and 2 1/2 is   12.____

   A. 15 1/4   B. 13 1/2   C. 12   D. 10 1/4

13. Most explosions in furnaces with oil-fired units result from *failure* to detect a   13.____

   A. dropping boiler pressure
   B. dropping steam temperature
   C. pulsating exit gas temperature
   D. loss of ignition

14. The MAIN reason why tools should NOT be left on catwalks or scaffolds is to   14.____

   A. prevent a mix-up of tools
   B. prevent the tools from being borrowed
   C. prevent damage to tools if they fell off onto the landing
   D. avoid a safety hazard

15. The proper extinguishing agent to use on a live electrical fire is   15.____

   A. carbon dioxide   B. steam
   C. water   D. foam

16. The FIRST procedure to follow upon witnessing smoke coming from an electronic control unit is to   16.____

   A. call the fire department
   B. pour water on it
   C. shut off the power
   D. look for a fire extinguisher

Questions 17-20.

DIRECTIONS: Questions 17 through 20 are to be answered SOLELY in accordance with the information contained in the following paragraph.

   Steel used in boiler construction must be of a higher quality than steel used in general construction. The boiler steel must be capable of sustaining loads at elevated temperatures. Temperature has a more serious effect upon the boiler fabrication than has the pressure. The material for bolts and studs is conditioned by tempering. The tempering temperature is at least 100° F higher than the service operating temperature. All materials used in boiler construction must be creep resistant to minimize the relaxation in service. Fire box quality plate is used for any part of a boiler exposed to the fire or products of combustion. For parts oi the boiler subject to pressure and not exposed to fire or products of combustion, flange quality plate is used. A small percentage of molybdenum is added to steel in the manufacture of superheater tubes, piping, and valves to increase the ability of these parts to withstand high temperature.

17. Material for bolts and studs used on boilers is conditioned for service by

    A. tempering   B. re-tightening
    C. forging   D. anodizing

17.___

18. The part of a boiler that is exposed to products of combustion is made of

    A. alloy materials   B. firebox quality plate
    C. flange quality plate   D. carbon steel

18.___

19. Temperature has a more serious effect upon boiler fabrication than has the

    A. vibration   B. steam
    C. relaxation   D. pressure

19.___

20. When comparing steel used in boiler construction to steel used in general construction, it can be said that steel used in boiler construction must be of a

    A. high-weld strength   B. low-carbon content
    C. lower quality   D. higher quality

20.___

KEY (CORRECT ANSWERS)

1.	D	11.	B
2.	D	12.	A
3.	C	13.	D
4.	D	14.	D
5.	C	15.	A
6.	A	16.	C
7.	D	17.	A
8.	D	18.	B
9.	C	19.	D
10.	A	20.	D

EXAMINATION SECTION
TEST 1

DIRECTIONS: Each question or incomplete statement is followed by several suggested answers or completions. Select the one that BEST answers the question or completes the statement. *PRINT THE LETTER OF THE CORRECT ANSWER IN THE SPACE AT THE RIGHT.*

1. The temperature at which water in an open vessel at sea level will boil is MOST NEARLY   1.____

   A. 100° F   B. 180° F   C. 212° F   D. 300° F

2. The fraction 3/8, expressed as a decimal, is   2.____

   A. 0.250   B. 0.281   C. 0.375   D. 0.406

3. The process of removing water, dissolved solids, and sludge from a boiler is called   3.____

   A. blowing down   B. screening
   C. topping   D. feeding

4. The remote control switch for all of the oil burners in a boiler room should be located   4.____

   A. adjacent to the boiler
   B. at each entrance to the boiler room
   C. on the mezzanine of the boiler room
   D. on the side of the boiler nearest an exit door

5. Of the following, an electrical fire should be extinguished with a fire extinguisher containing   5.____

   A. carbon tetrachloride   B. foamite
   C. carbon dioxide   D. soda acid

6. A steam preheater is COMMONLY used to   6.____

   A. generate superheated steam
   B. heat boiler make-up water
   C. heat #6 fuel oil before burning
   D. heat atmospheric air prior to combustion

7. Atomization as it applies to boiler operation is the process of   7.____

   A. breaking up atoms to obtain nuclear energy
   B. breaking up fuel oil into fine particles
   C. vaporizing water into steam
   D. mixing air and steam

8. The purpose of the try-cocks on a boiler is PRIMARILY to   8.____

   A. drain water from the boiler
   B. check the gage glass reading
   C. drain water from the gage glass
   D. blow down the boiler

9. A receiver in a compressed air system is used PRIMARILY to   9.__

    A. cool the air
    B. store the air
    C. remove particles of dust from the air
    D. saturate the air with vapor

10. A gage that can be used to measure either positive pressure or vacuum is GENERALLY   10.__
called a _____ gage.

    A. pump   B. sight   C. compound   D. steam

11. With respect to heating systems, the MAIN purpose of using a thermostat in a room is to   11.__

    A. improve the efficiency of the oil burner
    B. increase the flow of heated air
    C. regulate the humidity
    D. regulate the temperature

12. An inter-cooler is a device USUALLY used on a   12.__

    A. refrigerator
    B. rotary gear pump
    C. centrifugal pump
    D. multistage air compressor

13. A boiler feed water regulator automatically regulates the _____ the boiler.   13.__

    A. supply of make-up water to
    B. temperature of the water being supplied to
    C. maximum water temperature in
    D. pressure of the water being supplied to

14. In the electrical trade, the term BX refers to   14.__

    A. amplifier hook-up wires
    B. insulated wires in a rigid conduit
    C. a cable consisting of insulated wires in a flexible metal tubing
    D. a cable consisting of insulated wires in a plastic outer covering

15. When threading pipe, the tool that holds the die is called a   15.__

    A. holder   B. stock   C. yawl   D. wedge

16. The PROPER tool to use to remove the burrs from the inside of a pipe is a   16.__

    A. chisel   B. file   C. cutter   D. reamer

17. The wrench which is MOST often used to make connections in the piping for a boiler is a   17.__

    A. pump pliers   B. gas pliers
    C. Stillson wrench   D. vise-grip pliers

18. If the combustion sensing device (lead sulphide cell) in a boiler installation does not *see* a flame, the boiler is automatically shut down by the closing of the 18.____

    A. breech damper
    B. magnetic oil valve
    C. primary air supply damper
    D. secondary air supply damper

19. A wrench that is COMMONLY used to tighten a nut where only a short swing of the wrench handle is possible is called a(n) _____ wrench. 19.____

    A. Stillson   B. monkey   C. ratchet   D. allen

20. A solenoid valve is GENERALLY operated by 20.____

    A. water temperature   B. water pressure
    C. electricity   D. oil pressure

21. The water hammer noise that is sometimes heard in the steam lines of a heating system is USUALLY caused by 21.____

    A. high steam pressure
    B. condensation in the steam
    C. impurities in the boiler water
    D. high flue gas temperatures

22. A sump system in a building is NORMALLY used to collect all boiler room waste water and move it into the house 22.____

    A. transfer pump   B. settling tank
    C. sewer   D. recirculation tank

23. A centrifugal pump is located above a sump pit. The type of valve that is installed on the end of the suction line to the pump to assure that the line is primed is called a _____ valve. 23.____

    A. needle   B. gate   C. globe   D. foot

24. A gag or clamp on a safety valve is GENERALLY used when 24.____

    A. making a hydrostatic test on a boiler
    B. testing the setting of the safety valve
    C. filling the boiler with water
    D. testing the quality of the water

25. The PRIME function of an electrical circuit breaker is similar to that of a 25.____

    A. capacitor   B. conductance
    C. switch   D. fuse

26. A valve that opens when a solenoid is energized and closes when it is de-energized is called a _____ valve. 26.____

    A. thermistor   B. magnetic
    C. thermostatic   D. pressure regulator

27. The device which stops the flow of fuel oil to an oil burner in case of primary air failure is GENERALLY known as a

    A. thermostat   B. vaporstat
    C. pressuretrol   D. low pressure cut-off

27.__

28. A device that is used to start the operation of high voltage electrical equipment by means of a low voltage control circuit is called a

    A. relay   B. Wheatstone bridge
    C. Hartley circuit   D. thermocouple

28.__

29. A pyrometer can be used to measure the

    A. temperature of flue gas
    B. pressure of fuel oil
    C. percentage of CO_2 in flue gas
    D. amount of soot in flue gas

29.__

30. The low water cut-off in a boiler is USUALLY controlled by means of a

    A. bimetallic strip   B. float
    C. relay   D. bellows

30.__

31. The type of pump COMMONLY used to pump No. 6 fuel oil from the storage oil tanks is a(n) _____ pump.

    A. centrifugal   B. reciprocating
    C. gear   D. axial

31.__

32. One of the uses of a pressuretrol on a fuel oil fired steam boiler is to

    A. control the water pressure so that it is equal to the steam pressure
    B. prevent the steam pressure from exceeding a set value
    C. control the pressure of the fuel oil so that it does not exceed the relief valve setting
    D. control the pressure of the condensate to the vacuum pump

32.__

33. The GREATEST safety hazard of storing oily rags is that they can

    A. cause a fire   B. cause a foul odor
    C. produce toxic fumes   D. attract vermin

33.__

34. Of the following, the BEST action to take if you find a small puddle of oil on the boiler room floor is to

    A. ignore it   B. mop it up
    C. tell your supervisor   D. cover it with sawdust

34.__

35. When a long ladder is placed against a high wall, a rope should be tied from the lowest rung to the wall.
This is done to prevent

    A. anyone from walking under the ladder
    B. the ladder from slipping
    C. the rungs of the ladder from breaking
    D. someone from removing the ladder

35.__

36. Your fellow worker lifts one end of a piece of heavy equipment with a crowbar to permit   36.____
    you to work under this equipment with your hands.
    The PROPER safe procedure that you should follow is to

    A. insert temporary support blocks
    B. complete the job rapidly
    C. use heavy leather gloves
    D. lash the handle of the crowbar

37. Regulations require that domestic hot water should be supplied between the hours of   37.____

    A. 6:00 A.M. to 6:00 P.M.
    B. 6:00 A.M. to 12:00 Midnight
    C. 8:00 A.M. to 10:00 P.M.
    D. 12:00 Noon to 12:00 Midnight

38. In a fire tube boiler, it is MOST important to remove the soot from the   38.____

    A. outside surface of the tubes
    B. inside surface of the tubes
    C. walls of the combustion chamber
    D. intermediate tube sheet

39. A steam heating boiler is classified as a low pressure boiler when it generates steam at a   39.____
    gage pressure

    A. between 50 and 70 pounds per square inch
    B. between 30 and 50 pounds per square inch
    C. of 30 pounds per square inch or less
    D. of 15 pounds per square inch or less

40. The safety valve which is found on a steam boiler is designed to prevent the _____ from   40.____
    becoming too high.

    A. stack temperature   B. water level
    C. steam pressure   D. oil supply pressure

KEY (CORRECT ANSWERS)

1. C	11. D	21. B	31. C
2. C	12. D	22. C	32. B
3. A	13. A	23. D	33. A
4. B	14. C	24. A	34. B
5. C	15. B	25. D	35. B
6. C	16. D	26. B	36. A
7. B	17. C	27. B	37. B
8. B	18. B	28. A	38. B
9. B	19. C	29. A	39. D
10. C	20. C	30. B	40. C

TEST 2

DIRECTIONS: Each question or incomplete statement is followed by several suggested answers or completions. Select the one that BEST answers the question or completes the statement. *PRINT THE LETTER OF THE CORRECT ANSWER IN THE SPACE AT THE RIGHT.*

1. From the standpoint of corrosion resistance and reliability, the PREFERRED material for domestic hot water pipes from among the following is   1.__

    A. lead   B. brass   C. steel   D. plastic

2. The packing which is GENERALLY found in the stuffing box of a centrifugal water pump is used to   2.__

    A. reduce bearing wear
    B. reduce noise
    C. prevent leakage of water
    D. compensate for shaft misalignment

3. The MAIN function of a steam trap is to   3.__

    A. remove condensate from a steam supply line
    B. restrict the flow of steam in a supply line
    C. filter dirt out of a condensate return line
    D. remove steam from a water line

4. The sum of 2'6", 0'3", and 3'1" is   4.__

    A. 2'9"   B. 5'7"   C. 5'10"   D. 15'0"

5. A union is a plumbing fitting that is MOST commonly used to join   5.__

    A. two pieces of threaded pipe of the same diameter
    B. two pieces of threaded pipe of different diameter
    C. a gate valve to a threaded pipe
    D. an angle valve to a gate valve

6. A drain valve is used on a compressed air tank for the purpose of   6.__

    A. protecting the tank against excessively high pressures
    B. removing condensed vapor from the tank
    C. preventing air leakage from the tank
    D. starting the compressor

7. A valve which permits fluid to flow only in one direction in a pipe is called a _____ valve.   7.__

    A. needle   B. gate   C. globe   D. check

8. The shade or color of the smoke emitted from burning fuel oil in a burner can be compared to a standard chart called a _____ chart.   8.__

    A. Neumann   B. Ringelmann
    C. Mann   D. Kirchoff

9. The three MOST important pollutants which come from burning fuel oil are: particulates,   9.____
carbon monoxide, and

  A. oxygen   B. carbon dioxide
  C. sulphur dioxide   D. nitrogen

10. Number 6 fuel oil must be preheated before burning to   10.____

  A. reduce its viscosity
  B. increase its viscosity
  C. make use of excess steam
  D. make use of excess electricity

11. The deposits on the rotary oil cup of a burner should be cleaned with   11.____

  A. a file   B. a metal scraper
  C. kerosene and a rag   D. emery cloth

12. The low-water cut-off on a boiler should be tested by   12.____

  A. *lowering* the water level slowly
  B. *raising* the water level slowly
  C. *increasing* the firing rate
  D. *lowering* the firing rate

13. One POSSIBLE cause of smoke from an oil-fired boiler is   13.____

  A. contaminated boiler water
  B. low setting of the boiler relief valve
  C. low level of water in the boiler
  D. cold oil

14. The combustion efficiency of an oil-fired boiler can be determined from a combination of   14.____
the _____ temperature and the percentage of _____ in the flue gas.

  A. flue gas; oxygen   B. flue gas; carbon dioxide
  C. steam; oxygen   D. steam; carbon monoxide

15. A relief valve is usually placed on the discharge side of the positive displacement fuel oil   15.____
pump used to pump oil from the tank to the burner.
The MAIN purpose of this relief valve is to

  A. increase the flow of oil to the burner
  B. increase the temperature of the fuel oil
  C. remove entrapped air
  D. protect the oil pump

16. To insure proper burning, the No. 6 fuel oil going to the oil burner is heated to a tempera-   16.____
ture that is MOST NEARLY

  A. 220° F   B. 180° F   C. 140° F   D. 100° F

17. The device that regulates the amount of steam flowing through a fuel oil steam preheater   17.____
is called a

A. fuel oil pressure valve
B. fuel oil volume flow meter
C. steam volume flow meter
D. steam temperature regulator valve

18. Of the following materials, the one that is considered to have the BEST heat insulation property for a given thickness is

18.___

    A. wood
    C. copper
    B. glass wool
    D. steel

19. The function of the modutrol motor on a boiler is to

19.___

    A. open and close the fuel oil metering valve at the oil burner
    B. open and close the flow of fuel oil to the fuel oil heater
    C. control the flow of fuel oil from the storage tank
    D. control the flow of gas to ignite the fuel

20. The ignition system for an oil burner that burns No. 6 oil NORMALLY consists of a transformer, insulated electrodes and a(n)

20.___

    A. magnetic gas valve
    C. thermometer
    B. oil valve
    D. flow meter

21. A combustion sensing device, such as a lead sulfide cell, will close the magnetic valve feeding oil to the burner if it does not see a flame in APPROXIMATELY _____ to _____ seconds.

21.___

    A. $1; 1\frac{1}{2}$
    B. $2; 4$
    C. $4\frac{1}{2}; 6$
    D. $8; 16$

22. Bimetallic elements are NORMALLY found in _____ devices.

22.___

    A. pressure control
    C. pressure relief
    B. temperature control
    D. water level control

23. The cold oil interlock which prevents the oil burner from starting if the oil is too cold for proper smoke-free operation is located in the

23.___

    A. oil tank
    C. oil pump
    B. oil burner
    D. electric oil heater

24. The air flow interlock which will prevent the fuel oil valve from opening if there is no air pressure is located

24.___

    A. in the oil cup
    B. on top of the fan casing
    C. in the flue stack
    D. in the combustion chamber

25. A dirty or damaged oil cup in a rotary cup burner is MOST likely to cause

25.___

    A. poor mixing of oil and air
    B. an increase in oil flow
    C. an increase in oil pressure
    D. a decrease in air flow

26. The burner and boiler should each be inspected, cleaned, and overhauled _____ year(s).

    A. at least once a   B. once every two
    C. once every three   D. once every five

26.____

27. The accuracy of a fuel oil tank capacity gage is checked with a

    A. weighing scale   B. pressure gage
    C. density meter   D. dip stick

27.____

28. Vacuum tubes in oil burner control devices must be replaced even if they are in operating condition once every _____ months.

    A. 3   B. 6   C. 12   D. 18

28.____

29. The soot blower used to blow soot out of the boiler tubes must be operated ONLY

    A. when the oil burner is shut down for at least 30 minutes
    B. when the oil burner is in operation
    C. when the oil burner is removed
    D. prior to operation of the burner

29.____

30. The pipe that leads from the storage oil tank to the outside of the building and which is at least 2 feet above the curb line and open to the atmosphere is called a _____ line.

    A. vent   B. fill
    C. oil depth check   D. suction

30.____

31. The device used to regulate draft in a furnace is called a

    A. damper B. stay bolt C. bonnet D. mudring

31.____

32. The secondary air damper is located under the burner, and the APPROXIMATE percentage of the total air that this damper supplies for complete fuel combustion is

    A. 30%   B. 45%   C. 70%   D. 85%

32.____

33. The color that is MOST commonly used to identify a fire standpipe is

    A. bright red   B. black
    C. bright blue   D. silver gray

33.____

34. The device that starts and stops the sump pump at predetermined water levels in the sump pit is called a _____ switch.

    A. float   B. micro
    C. double pole   D. single pole

34.____

Questions 35-40.

DIRECTIONS: Questions 35 through 40, inclusive, are based on the paragraph *Hot Water Generation* shown below. When answering these questions, refer ONLY to this paragraph.

HOT WATER GENERATION

The hot water that comes from a faucet is called Domestic Hot Water.

It is heated by a steam coil that runs through a storage tank full of water in the basement of each building.

As the tenants take the hot water, fresh cold water enters the tank and is heated. The temperature of this water is automatically kept at approximately 140° F.

The device which controls the temperature is called a temperature regulator valve. It is operated by a bellows, capillary tube, and thermo bulb which connects between the valve and the hot water being stored in the tank. This bulb, tube, and bellows contains a liquid which expands and contracts with changes in temperature.

As the water in the tank reaches 140° F, the liquid in the thermo bulb expands and causes pressure to travel along the capillary tube and into the bellows. The expanded liquid forces the bellows to push the Temperature Regulator Valve Stem down, closing the valve. No more steam can enter the coil in the tank, and the water will get no hotter.

As the hot water is used by the tenants, cold water enters the tank and pulls the temperature down. This causes the liquid in the thermo bulb to cool and contract (shrink). The pressure is no longer in the bellows and a spring pushes it up, allowing the valve to open and allowing steam to again enter the heating coil in the storage tank raising the temperature of the Domestic Hot Water to 140° F.

35. Domestic hot water is heated by   35.__

    A. coal   B. electricity
    C. hot water   D. steam

36. The temperature of domestic hot water is MOST NEARLY   36.__

    A. 75° F   B. 100° F   C. 140° F   D. 212° F

37. The temperature of the hot water is controlled by a   37.__

    A. thermometer
    B. temperature regulator valve
    C. pressuretrol
    D. pressure gauge

38. The temperature regulator valve is operated by a combination of a   38.__

    A. thermometer and a thermo bulb
    B. thermometer and a pyrometer
    C. bellows, capillary tube, and a thermometer
    D. bellows, capillary tube, and a thermo bulb

39. Closing of the temperature regulator valve prevents _____ from entering the heating   39.__
    coil in the tank.

    A. water   B. steam
    C. electricity   D. air

40. As hot water is used by the tenants, the temperature of the water in the tank   40.____

    A. increases   B. decreases
    C. remains the same   D. approaches 212° F

KEY (CORRECT ANSWERS)

1.	B	11.	C	21.	B	31.	A
2.	C	12.	A	22.	B	32.	D
3.	A	13.	D	23.	D	33.	A
4.	C	14.	B	24.	B	34.	A
5.	A	15.	D	25.	A	35.	D
6.	B	16.	B	26.	A	36.	C
7.	D	17.	D	27.	D	37.	B
8.	B	18.	B	28.	C	38.	D
9.	C	19.	A	29.	B	39.	B
10.	A	20.	A	30.	A	40.	B

EXAMINATION SECTION
TEST 1

DIRECTIONS: Each question or incomplete statement is followed by several suggested answers or completions. Select the one that BEST answers the question or completes the statement. *PRINT THE LETTER OF THE CORRECT ANSWER IN THE SPACE AT THE RIGHT.*

1. Of the following classifications of fuel oils, the one which is NO longer made is   1._____

    A. #1   B. #2   C. #3   D. #6

2. Water at sea level and atmospheric pressure in an open container will boil at a temperature of   2._____

    A. 238° F   B. 212° F   C. 190° F   D. 172° F

3. A gauge pressure of 6.1 psi is equivalent to an absolute pressure of MOST NEARLY _____ psia.   3._____

    A. 30   B. 26   C. 21   D. 16

4. A pyrometer is used to measure   4._____

    A. draft   B. resistance
    C. temperature   D. velocity

5. Furnace draft is USUALLY measured in   5._____

    A. cubic feet   B. feet of mercury
    C. inches of air   D. inches of water

6. An ORSAT apparatus is used in a boiler plant to analyze   6._____

    A. feedwater   B. flue gas
    C. fuel   D. smoke haze

7. The device that prevents explosions in oil-fired boilers due to flame failure is the   7._____

    A. mercury tube   B. light sensing unit
    C. electrical transformer   D. limit switch

8. The water level in a boiler operating 24 hours a day should be checked   8._____

    A. every 8 hours   B. once every 16 hours
    C. weekly   D. once every month

9. The boiler and oil burner should be inspected, overhauled, and cleaned at least once every   9._____

    A. 3 years   B. 18 months
    C. year   D. month

10. The PROPER procedure to follow when taking a boiler out of service is to   10._____

    A. *reduce* the fuel feed and slowly decrease the output
    B. *increase* the fuel feed and open all dampers

C.   *open* all water supply valves and drain the boiler
D.   *increase* the steam pressure and burn all the fuel

11. In the city, health regulations require domestic hot water to be supplied to tenants only between the hours of   11.__

   A.   6:00 A.M. to 12:00 Midnight
   B.   8:00 A.M. to 8:00 P.M.
   C.   12:00 Noon to 12:00 Midnight
   D.   10:00 A.M. to 6:00 P.M.

12. In an efficiently operated heating plant, the flue gas temperature should be APPROXI-MATELY   12.__

   A.   150° F   B.   200° F   C.   350° F   D.   800° F

13. For MAXIMUM heat efficiency in a fire tube boiler, soot must be removed from the   13.__

   A.   lifting rings
   B.   outer tube surfaces
   C.   walls of the crown sheet
   D.   inner surface of the tubes

14. The percentage of carbon dioxide in the flue gas of an efficiently operated boiler should be APPROXIMATELY   14.__

   A.   4%   B.   6%   C.   12%   D.   18%

15. The combustion efficiency of a boiler is indicated by the amount of carbon dioxide in the flue gas and the   15.__

   A.   size of the stack
   B.   quality of the fuel
   C.   temperature of the combustion air
   D.   temperature of the flue gas

16. The pH value of boiler feedwater is normally MOST NEARLY kept at   16.__

   A.   3   B.   6   C.   10   D.   13

17. The one of the following that is used in the internal treatment of boiler feedwater to increase alkalinity is   17.__

   A.   oxygen   B.   tannin
   C.   sodium alginate   D.   soda ash

18. Of the following types of pumps, the one that is MOST commonly used with gun-type oil burners is the   18.__

   A.   external or internal gear pump
   B.   volute type
   C.   centrifugal type
   D.   propeller type

19. The hole in a direct-contact fire-actuated plug as used in a boiler is USUALLY filled with   19.____

    A. brass   B. lead   C. carbon   D. tin

20. The MAIN reason why soot blowers must be used only when the oil burners are in operation is to   20.____

    A. prevent a possible explosion
    B. reduce air pollution
    C. maintain building temperatures
    D. increase the boiler water temperature

21. The boiler low water cut-off is controlled by a   21.____

    A. relay   B. float   C. diaphragm   D. spring

22. The boiler connection from the last pass to the breech is called the   22.____

    A. drypan   B. rear tube
    C. safety outlet   D. bonnet

23. The function of a condensation pump in a steam system is to   23.____

    A. direct condensate to the house sewer
    B. prime the boiler
    C. condense steam to water
    D. return hot condensate to the boiler

24. A steam heating system that operates under both vacuum and low pressure conditions without the use of a vacuum pump is called a(n) _____ system.   24.____

    A. air   B. vapor   C. vacuum   D. water

25. A hot water heating boiler is classified as a low pressure boiler when it makes hot water at a gauge pressure NOT more than _____ psi.   25.____

    A. 300   B. 260   C. 200   D. 160

26. The one of the following gauge pressures that is MOST characteristic of a low pressure steam boiler is _____ psi.   26.____

    A. 30   B. 25   C. 20   D. 10

27. In the event of low water in a boiler, the burner will be shut down by the   27.____

    A. ignition transformer
    B. low water cut-off
    C. centrifugal switch on the burner
    D. damper control

28. A fuel oil steam preheater is USUALLY equipped with a   28.____

    A. mudring device
    B. steam temperature regulating valve
    C. steam volume gage
    D. boiler water level indicator

29. The MAIN function of a steam trap in a boiler heating system is to   29.__

    A. collect sediment from the steam lines
    B. return heat from the hot water to the building
    C. lower the temperature of the steam
    D. collect the water of condensation from steam apparatus

30. The one of the following which is a device that prevents the steam pressure in an oil-fired boiler from rising above a specified value is the   30.__

    A. pressuretrol   B. magnetic oil valve
    C. haze gauge   D. vaporstat

31. The type of valve used in feedwater lines where flow in only one direction is required is   31.__

    A. stop   B. gate   C. plug   D. check

32. The device that is used to force water into a boiler operating under pressure is the   32.__

    A. duplex   B. slide valve
    C. rocker arm   D. injector

33. The function of a feedwater heater in a boiler plant is to   33.__

    A. generate hot water for the building
    B. regulate the hot water temperature
    C. heat and condition water for the boiler
    D. condition chemicals for water leaving the boiler

34. A hot water heating system has an expansion tank to compensate for changes in the   34.__

    A. volume of water in the system
    B. volume of steam in the system
    C. water treatment process
    D. piping runs due to expansion of the metal pipe

35. One gallon of potable water weighs APPROXIMATELY _____ lbs.   35.__

    A. 6.8   B. 7.5   C. 8.3   D. 9.6

36. The bridge wall in a heating boiler is located   36.__

    A. above the arch
    B. in the steam drum
    C. behind the grates
    D. at the base of the chimney

37. A clamp or gag on a safety valve is generally used ONLY when   37.__

    A. testing a boiler hydrostatically
    B. surface-blowing the boiler
    C. adding chemicals to the feedwater
    D. cleaning the oil burner

38. Make-up water to a boiler is automatically controlled by the

    A. boiler water temperature
    B. boiler pressure
    C. metering valve
    D. feedwater regulator

38.____

39. Try-cocks are installed on a boiler for

    A. relieving air pressure in the system
    B. indicating the water level in the boiler
    C. blowing out the excess water from the boiler
    D. draining the water column

39.____

40. Steam preheaters are USUALLY used in an oil burning installation to

    A. preheat boiler feedwater
    B. add heat to saturated steam
    C. raise the temperature of the flue gas
    D. heat the fuel oil before it enters the burner

40.____

KEY (CORRECT ANSWERS)

1.	C	11.	A	21.	B	31.	D
2.	B	12.	C	22.	D	32.	D
3.	C	13.	D	23.	D	33.	C
4.	C	14.	C	24.	B	34.	A
5.	D	15.	D	25.	D	35.	C
6.	B	16.	C	26.	D	36.	C
7.	B	17.	D	27.	B	37.	A
8.	A	18.	A	28.	B	38.	D
9.	C	19.	D	29.	D	39.	B
10.	A	20.	A	30.	A	40.	D

TEST 2

Each question or incomplete statement is followed by several suggested answers or completions. Select the one that BEST answers the question or completes the statement. *PRINT THE LETTER OF THE CORRECT ANSWER IN THE SPACE AT THE RIGHT.*

1. The temperature in a heated room can be regulated by a

    A. trap   B. scanner   C. damper   D. thermostat

1.__

2. Impurities and solids are removed from boiler water by a procedure known as

    A. screening   B. blowing down
    C. priming   D. foaming

2.__

3. To throttle the flow of steam in a steam line, use a

    A. brass mounting   B. gate valve
    C. globe valve   D. union

3.__

4. A highly objectionable air pollutant of fuel oil is

    A. nitrogen   B. carbon   C. hydrogen   D. sulphur

4.__

5. The modutrol motor on an oil-fired boiler controls the

    A. primary air damper
    B. gas flow for ignition
    C. oil returning to the fuel tank
    D. safety gauge

5.__

6. The one of the following that stops the flow of oil to the spinning cup of a rotary cup oil burner is the

    A. metering valve   B. magnetic oil valve
    C. regulating valve   D. fan casing

6.__

7. The one of the following that stops the flow of fuel oil to a rotary cup oil burner in the event of primary air failure is the

    A. vaporstat   B. electrode
    C. primary air damper   D. gas stop valve

7.__

8. In a rotary cup oil burner, the breaking up of the fuel oil into fine droplets is known as

    A. aeration   B. vaporization
    C. atomization   D. injection

8.__

9. The one of the following devices that controls the fuel oil temperature leaving the oil heater is the

    A. oil interlock   B. strainer
    C. aquastat   D. suction valve

9.__

10. Of the following causes of smoke in oil-burning installations, the one which occurs MOST   10._____
frequently is

    A. faulty atomization due to insufficient preheat
    B. insufficient draft loss through the boiler
    C. insufficient air due to lack of draft
    D. too much oil being fed into a cold furnace on starting

11. The stack switch shuts off the oil to an oil burner in the event of   11._____

    A. an air pollution alert
    B. excessive boiler pressures
    C. on oversupply of fuel
    D. flame failure

12. In the city, the Ringelmann Chart is used to determine the density of   12._____

    A. smoke   B. coal   C. fuel oil   D. water

13. A centrifugal pump is MAINLY packed to   13._____

    A. prevent water leakage   B. lubricate the bearings
    C. reduce heat   D. prevent noise

14. The BEST procedure to follow when lubricating a pump is to apply lubricant   14._____

    A. only if needed
    B. on a regular schedule
    C. whenever you think the lubricant is low
    D. only when the pump is shut down

15. When pumping water out of a pit, the one of the following that should be installed on the   15._____
suction end of the line is a

    A. foot valve   B. throttle valve
    C. volute   D. governor

16. The ASME Boiler Code is used for rating boilers. The letters ASME are an abbreviation   16._____
for

    A. Allied for Standards of Mechanical Engineers
    B. American Society of Mechanical Engineers
    C. American Steam Maintenance Engineers
    D. American Society of Methods Engineers

17. The function of a sump pump in a boiler room is to collect boiler room drips and dis-   17._____
charge it into the

    A. transfer tank   B. nearest public street
    C. conditioning tank   D. house sewer

18. Of the following instruments, the one that is used to measure atmospheric pressure is   18._____
a(n)

    A. odometer   B. thermometer
    C. barometer   D. manometer

19. A compound gauge measures

    A. humidity and vacuum   B. temperature and pressure
    C. pressure and vibration   D. pressure and vacuum

19.___

20. An inter-cooler would GENERALLY be installed on a(n)

    A. air compressor   B. rotary gear pump
    C. fuel tank   D. evaporator

20.___

21. The one of the following that is BEST to use to loosen a rusted bolt is

    A. penetrating oil   B. engine oil
    C. graphite   D. silica

21.___

22. The one of the following that is used to thread a pipe externally is called a

    A. guide   B. die   C. stock   D. tap

22.___

23. A frequent cause of knocking in low-pressure steam lines is

    A. condensation of the steam
    B. an increase of steam temperature
    C. high water temperature
    D. insufficient fuel supply

23.___

24. Viscosity is a measure of the resistance of a fuel oil to

    A. burning   B. flowing
    C. vaporization   D. deterioration

24.___

25. The PROPER procedure to follow for safety when working on a ladder is to

    A. not face the ladder when descending
    B. use a sturdy object to obtain additional ladder height
    C. take one step at a time when ascending or descending a ladder
    D. always have two men on the ladder at the same time

25.___

26. Oily waste rags should be kept in a closed metal container MAINLY to

    A. prevent fire
    B. keep the rags from drying out
    C. eliminate attraction to bugs
    D. prevent oil seepage onto the floor

26.___

27. Fire standpipe systems are GENERALLY painted

    A. black   B. red   C. blue   D. white

27.___

28. The oil burner remote control switch should be located

    A. on the front of the boiler
    B. on the stack of the boiler
    C. at the control panel
    D. at each entrance to the boiler room

28.___

29. Insulated electrical wire in flexible metal tubing is known as   29.____

    A. BX   B. cable   C. RX   D. conduit

30. The one of the following that is used to measure air pressure is a   30.____

    A. calorimeter   B. venturi
    C. compensator   D. manometer

31. Pressures below atmospheric are USUALLY expressed in   31.____

    A. pounds of air   B. inches of water
    C. inches of mercury   D. pounds of steam

32. The reading of the fuel oil tank capacity gauge is checked by using a   32.____

    A. steam nozzle   B. dip stick
    C. drip pan   D. pressure gauge

33. In piping systems, nominal size refers to   33.____

    A. outside diameter   B. length in feet
    C. inside diameter   D. weight in pounds

34. The one of the following plumbing fittings which is used to connect two pieces of the   34.____
same diameter threaded pipe is a

    A. cap   B. bushing   C. union   D. plug

35. A four-inch-long galvanized pipe having a diameter of one inch and male threads at both   35.____
ends is called a(n)

    A. nipple   B. turnbuckle
    C. elbow   D. coupling

36. A galvanized flue pipe with an outside diameter of seven inches will have a circumfer-   36.____
ence in inches of MOST NEARLY equal to

    A. 22   B. 20   C. 19   D. 17

37. The sum of 2.6", 1.2", and 4.1" is   37.____

    A. 6.6"   B. 7.3"   C. 7.9"   D. 8.2"

38. An electric motor is NORMALLY rated in   38.____

    A. ohms   B. farads
    C. horsepower   D. megawatts

39. The one of the following electrical devices which USUALLY contains a magnetic coil is   39.____
the

    A. battery   B. thermocouple
    C. relay   D. fustat

40. The MOST important requirement of a good boiler room report is that it should be   40._

   A. prepared quickly
   B. short and clear
   C. very long and detailed
   D. shown to the building tenants

_____

KEY (CORRECT ANSWERS)

1.	D	11.	D	21.	A	31.	C
2.	B	12.	A	22.	B	32.	B
3.	C	13.	A	23.	A	33.	A
4.	D	14.	B	24.	B	34.	C
5.	A	15.	A	25.	C	35.	A
6.	B	16.	B	26.	A	36.	A
7.	A	17.	D	27.	B	37.	C
8.	C	18.	C	28.	D	38.	C
9.	C	19.	D	29.	A	39.	C
10.	D	20.	A	30.	D	40.	B

_____

EXAMINATION SECTION
TEST 1

DIRECTIONS: Each question or incomplete statement is followed by several suggested answers or completions. Select the one that BEST answers the question or completes the Statement. *PRINT THE LETTER OF THE CORRECT ANSWER IN THE SPACE AT THE RIGHT.*

1. The bottom blowdown on a boiler is used to   1.____

   A. remove mud drum water impurities
   B. increase boiler priming
   C. reduce steam pressure in the header
   D. increase the boiler water level

2. The term *spalling* refers to a boiler   2.____

   A. flue gas content   B. soot blower
   C. combustion chamber   D. mud leg

3. The wrench that would normally be used on hexagonally-shaped screwed valves and fit-   3.____
   tings is the _____ wrench.

   A. adjustable pipe   B. tappet
   C. monkey   D. open-end

4. The designated size of a boiler tube is GENERALLY based upon its   4.____

   A. internal diameter
   B. external diameter
   C. wall thickness
   D. weight per foot of length

5. A fusible plug on a boiler is made PRIMARILY of   5.____

   A. selenium   B. tin   C. zinc   D. iron

6. The range of pH values for boiler feed water is NORMALLY   6.____

   A. 1 to 2   B. 4 to 6   C. 9 to 10   D. 12 to 15

7. The *boiler horsepower* is defined as the evaporation of _____ lbs. of water from and at   7.____
   212° F.

   A. 900   B. 400   C. 345   D. 34.5

8. A low pressure air-atomizing oil burner has an operating air pressure range of _____   8.____
   lbs.

   A. 25 to 35   B. 16 to 20   C. 6 to 10   D. 1 to 2

9. A superheater is installed in a Stirling boiler MAINLY for the purpose of raising the tem-   9.____
   perature of the

   A. secondary air   B. steam leaving the steam drum
   C. boiler feed water   D. primary air

10. The function of a counterflow economizer in a power plant is to   10.__

    A. use flue gases to heat feedwater
    B. raise flue gas temperatures
    C. recirculate exhaust steam
    D. pre-heat combustion air

11. A fire due to spontaneous combustion would MOST easily occur in a pile of   11.__

    A. asbestos sheathing   B. loose lumber
    C. oil drums   D. oily waste rags

12. A *damper regulator,* used for combustion control, is operated by   12.__

    A. steam pressure   B. the water column
    C. the boiler pump   D. a pitot tube

13. The packing of an expansion joint in a firebrick wall of a combustion chamber is GENER-   13.__
ALLY made of

    A. silica   B. brick cement
    C. silicon carbide   D. asbestos

14. An open-ended steam pipe, called a steam lance, is USUALLY used on a boiler to   14.__

    A. remove soot   B. bleed the steam header
    C. clean the mud drum   D. clean chimneys

15. A high vacuum reading on the fuel oil gauge would indicate   15.__

    A. an empty oil tank   B. high oil temperature
    C. a clogged strainer   D. worn pump gears

16. The one of the following boilers that is classified as an internally fired boiler is the _____   16.__
boiler.

    A. cross-drum straight tube
    B. vertical tubular
    C. Stirling
    D. cross-drum horizontal box-header

17. Try-cocks are used on a boiler PRIMARILY to   17.__

    A. check the gauge glass reading
    B. release steam pressure
    C. drain the water column
    D. blow down the gauge glass

18. Scale deposits on the tubes and shell of a high-pressure boiler are UNDESIRABLE   18.__
because the deposits cause

    A. protrusions or roughness   B. suction
    C. foaming   D. concentrates

19. The function of a radiation pyrometer is to measure

19._____

    A. boiler water height   B. boiler pressure
    C. furnace temperature   D. boiler drum stresses

20. An engine indicator is GENERALLY used to measure

20._____

    A. steam temperature
    B. heat losses
    C. errors in gauge readings
    D. steam cylinder pressures

21. A goose-neck is installed in the line connecting a steam gauge to a boiler to

21._____

    A. maintain constant steam flow
    B. prevent steam knocking
    C. maintain steam pressure
    D. protect the gauge element

22. A boiler steam gauge should have a range of AT LEAST

22._____

    A. one-half the working steam pressure
    B. the working steam pressure
    C. 1 1/2 times the maximum allowable working pressure
    D. twice the maximum allowable working pressure

23. A disconnected steam pressure gauge is USUALLY calibrated with a(n)

23._____

    A. Orsat instrument   B. air pump
    C. tuyeres   D. dead-weight tester

24. The recommended size joint for repairing firebrick wall is MOST nearly

24._____

    A. 1/64"   B. 1/16"   C. 1/4"   D. 1/2"

25. The acidity of boiler water is USUALLY determined by a _____ test.

25._____

    A. Rockwell   B. soap hardness
    C. paper   D. alkalinity

26. Electrostatic precipitators are used in power plants to

26._____

    A. remove fly ash from flue gases
    B. measure smoke conditions
    C. collect boiler impurities
    D. disperse minerals in feed water

27. Fly ash from the flue gases in a power plant is collected by a

27._____

    A. soot blower   B. gas separator
    C. stack regulator   D. mechanical separator

28. The installation of four new split packing rings in a stuffing box requires that the joints of the packing rings be placed _____° apart.

    A. 180   B. 90   C. 60   D. 30

28.____

29. In power plants, boiler feed water is chemically treated in order to

    A. prevent scale formation
    B. increase water foaming
    C. increase oxygen formation
    D. increase the temperature of the water

29.____

30. The soot in a fire tube boiler GENERALLY settles on the

    A. bridgewall
    B. inside tube surface
    C. combustion chamber sides
    D. outside tube surface

30.____

31. The one of the following classifications of fuel oil strainers that is generally NOT used with the heavier industrial fuel oils is a _____ strainer.

    A. wire mesh
    B. metallic disc
    C. filter cloth
    D. perforated metal cylinder

31.____

32. The temperature of the fuel oil leaving a pre-heater is controlled by a(n)

    A. potentiometer   B. relay
    C. low water cut-off   D. aquastat

32.____

33. A pneumatic tool is GENERALLY powered by

    A. natural gas   B. steam
    C. a battery   D. air

33.____

34. In the city, the maximum steam pressure permitted in the steam coils used for heating the oil in a submerged oil storage tank is MOST NEARLY _____ Psi.

    A. 40   B. 35   C. 25   D. 10

34.____

35. The water pressure used in a hydrostatic test on a boiler is GENERALLY _____ maximum working pressure.

    A. 4 times the   B. 2 times the
    C. 1 1/2 times the   D. the same as

35.____

36. The one of the following valves that should be used in a steam line to throttle the flow is the _____ valve.

    A. plug   B. check   C. gate   D. globe

36.____

37. The CO (carbon monoxide) content in the flue gas from an efficiently fired boiler should be APPROXIMATELY

    A. 0% to 1%   B. 4% to 6%   C. 8% to 10%   D. 12% to 13%

37.____

38. The CO_2 (carbon dioxide) percentage in the flue gas of an efficiently fired boiler should be APPROXIMATELY   38.____

    A. 1%   B. 12%   C. 18%   D. 25%

39. When the temperature of stack gases rises considerably above the normal operating stack temperature, it GENERALLY indicates   39.____

    A. a low boiler water level
    B. a heavy smoke condition in the stack
    C. that the boiler is operating efficiently
    D. that the boiler tubes are dirty

40. A boiler safety valve is usually set above the maximum working pressure by an amount equal to _____% of the maximum working pressure.   40.____

    A. 6   B. 10   C. 12   D. 14

KEY (CORRECT ANSWERS)

1.	A	11.	D	21.	D	31.	C
2.	C	12.	A	22.	C	32.	D
3.	D	13.	D	23.	D	33.	D
4.	B	14.	A	24.	B	34.	D
5.	B	15.	C	25.	D	35.	C
6.	C	16.	B	26.	A	36.	D
7.	D	17.	A	27.	D	37.	A
8.	D	18.	A	28.	B	38.	B
9.	B	19.	C	29.	A	39.	D
10.	A	20.	D	30.	B	40.	A

TEST 2

DIRECTIONS: Each question or incomplete statement is followed by several suggested answers or completions. Select the one that BEST answers the question or completes the statement. *PRINT THE LETTER OF THE CORRECT ANSWER IN THE SPACE AT THE RIGHT.*

1. The one of the following grades of fuel oil that contains the GREATEST heating value, in BTU per gallon, is   1.___

    A. #2   B. #4   C. #5   D. #6

2. When we say that a fuel oil has a high viscosity, we mean MAINLY that the fuel oil will   2.___

    A. evaporate easily
    B. burn without smoke
    C. flow slowly through pipes
    D. have a low specific gravity

3. The type of fuel oil pump GENERALLY used with a rotary cup oil burner system is the _____ pump.   3.___

    A. propeller   B. internal
    C. centrifugal   D. piston

4. No. 6 fuel oil flowing to a mechanical atomizing burner should be preheated to APPROX-IMATELY _____° F.   4.___

    A. 185   B. 115   C. 100   D. 80

5. The flame of an industrial rotary cup oil burner should be adjusted so that the flame   5.___

    A. has a yellow color with blue spots
    B. strikes all sides of the combustion chamber
    C. has a light brown color
    D. does not strike the rear of the combustion chamber

6. The location of the oil burner *remote control switch* should GENERALLY be   6.___

    A. at the boiler room entrance
    B. on the boiler shell
    C. on the oil burner motor
    D. on a wall nearest the boiler

7. With forced draft, the approximate wind box pressure in a single-retort underfeed stoker is NORMALLY   7.___

    A. 2"   B. 5"   C. 7"   D. 9"

8. The pressure over the fire in a coal-fired steam boiler with a balanced-draft system and natural draft is MOST NEARLY   8.___

    A. +.60"   B. +.50"   C. -.02"   D. -.70"

9. Three tons of coal with an ash content of 10% will yield a weight of ash of MOST
   NEARLY _____ pounds.

    A. 400   B. 500   C. 600   D. 700

    9._____

10. To clean and spread the coal over the grates of a coal-fired boiler, a stationary fireman
    would use a tool known as a(n)

    10._____

    A. hoe   B. extractor
    C. lance   D. slice bar

11. To burn the volatile matter in coal more efficiently, one should

    11._____

    A. mix peat with the coal
    B. supply overfire draft
    C. mix it with a lower grade of coal
    D. add moisture to the coal

12. The one of the following that lists the size classifications of anthracite coal in proper order
    ranging from the smallest to the largest is

    12._____

    A. chestnut, culm, pea, birdseye, egg
    B. egg, stove, pea, broken, culm
    C. stove, egg, birdseye, culm, broken
    D. birdseye, pea, chestnut, stove, egg

13. The fire in a hand-fired furnace can be cleaned by a method known as

    13._____

    A. ashpit to grate   B. bottom to top
    C. side to side   D. grate to crown

14. Coal is normally *tempered* when operating a chain-grate stoker for the purpose of

    14._____

    A. increasing coking   B. preventing clinking
    C. collecting particles   D. promoting uniform burning

15. The one of the following coals that can legally be burned in city power plants is

    15._____

    A. anthracite   B. sub-bituminous
    C. non-coking   D. bituminous

16. The one of the following that is known as *rice coal* is

    16._____

    A. pea coal   B. buckwheat (No. 2 coal)
    C. egg coal   D. culm coal

17. A MAJOR cause of air pollution resulting from the burning of fuel oils is _____ dioxide.

    17._____

    A. sulphur   B. silicon   C. nitrous   D. hydrogen

18. The CO_2 percentage in the flue gas of a power plant is indicated by a

    18._____

    A. Doppler meter   B. Ranarex indicator
    C. Microtector   D. hygrometer

19. The MOST likely cause of black smoke exhausting from the chimney of an oil-fired boiler is

19.___

    A. high secondary air flow   B. low stack emission
    C. low oil temperature   D. high chimney draft

20. The diameter of the steam piston in a steam-driven duplex vacuum pump whose dimensions are given as 3 by 2 by 4 is

20.___

    A. 2   B. 3   C. 4   D. 6

21. An induced draft fan is GENERALLY connected between the

21.___

    A. condenser and the first pass
    B. stack and the breeching
    C. feedwater heater and the boiler feed pump
    D. combustion chamber and fuel oil tanks

22. The purpose of an air chamber on a reciprocating water pump is to

22.___

    A. maintain a uniform flow
    B. reduce the amount of steam expansion
    C. create a pulsating flow
    D. vary the amount of steam admission

23. *Flash point* is the temperature at which oil will

23.___

    A. change completely to vapor
    B. safely fire in a furnace
    C. flash into flame if a lighted match is passed just above the top of the oil
    D. burn intermittently when ignited

24. A *sounding box* would NORMALLY be found

24.___

    A. on top of the boiler
    B. next to a compressed air tank
    C. in a fuel oil tank
    D. in a steam condenser

25. An *intercooler* is GENERALLY found on a(n)

25.___

    A. steam pump   B. air compressor
    C. steam engine   D. rotary oil pump

26. The instrument used to measure atmospheric pressure is a

26.___

    A. capillary tube   B. venturi
    C. barometer   D. calorimeter

27. The control which starts or stops the operation of the oil burner at a predetermined steam pressure is the

27.___

    A. pressuretrol   B. air flow interlock
    C. transformer   D. magnetic oil valve

28. In a closed feedwater heater, the water and the steam   28.____

    A. come into direct contact
    B. are kept apart from each other
    C. are under negative pressure
    D. mix and exhaust to the atmosphere

29. A *knocking* noise in steam lines is GENERALLY the result of   29.____

    A. superheated steam expansion
    B. high steam pressure
    C. condensation in the line
    D. rapid steam expansion

30. An electrical component known as a step-up transformer operates by   30.____

    A. raising voltage and decreasing amperage
    B. decreasing amperage and raising resistance
    C. raising amperage and decreasing resistance
    D. raising voltage and amperage at the same time

31. A manometer is an instrument that is used to measure   31.____

    A. heat radiation   B. air volume
    C. condensate water level   D. air pressure

32. Three 75-gallon per hour mechanical pressure type oil burners operating together are to   32.____
burn 150,000 gallons of No. 6 fuel oil.
The number of hours they would take to burn this amount of oil is MOST NEARLY

    A. 665   B. 760   C. 870   D. 1210

33. The sum of 10 1/2, 8 3/4, 5 1/2, and 2 1/2 is   33.____

    A. 23   B. 25   C. 26   D. 27

34. A water tank measures 50 feet long, 16 feet wide, and 12 feet high. Assume that water   34.____
weighs 60 pounds per cubic foot and that one gallon of water weighs 8 pounds. The
number of gallons the tank can hold when it is half full is

    A. 21,500   B. 28,375   C. 33,410   D. 36,000

35. Assuming 70 gallons of oil cost $42.00, then 110 gallons of oil at the same rate will cost   35.____

    A. $66.00   B. $84.00   C. $96.00   D. $152.00

Questions 36-40.

DIRECTIONS: Questions 36 through 40 are to be answered on the basis of the information
contained in the following paragraph.

Fuel is conserved when a boiler is operating near its most efficient load. The efficiency of
a boiler will change as the output varies. Large amounts of air must be used at low ratings
and so the heat exchanger is inefficient. As the output increases, the efficiency decreases
due to an increase in flue gas temperature. Every boiler has an output rate for which its efficiency is highest. For example, in a water-tube boiler, the highest efficiency might occur at

120 percent of rated capacity while in a vertical fire-tube boiler highest efficiency might be at 70% of rated capacity.

The type of fuel burned and cleanliness affect the maximum efficiency of the boiler. When a power plant contains a battery of boilers, a sufficient number should be kept in operation so as to maintain the output of individual units near their points of maximum efficiency. One of the boilers in the battery can be used as a regulator to meet the change in demand for steam while the other boilers could still operate at their most efficient rating. Boiler performance is expressed as the number of pounds of steam generated per pound of fuel.

36. According to the above paragraph, the number of pounds of steam generated per pound of fuel is a measure of boiler 36.____

    A. size   B. performance
    C. regulator input   D. by-pass

37. According to the above paragraph, the HIGHEST efficiency of a vertical fire-tube boiler might occur at _____ capacity. 37.____

    A. 70% of rated   B. 80% of water tube
    C. 95% of water tube   D. 120% of rated

38. According to the above paragraph, the MAXIMUM efficiency of a boiler is affected by 38.____

    A. atmospheric temperature   B. atmospheric pressure
    C. cleanliness   D. fire brick material

39. According to the above paragraph, a heat exchanger uses large amounts of air at low 39.____

    A. fuel rates   B. ratings
    C. temperatures   D. pressures

40. According to the above paragraph, one boiler in a battery of boilers should be used as a 40.____

    A. demand   B. stand-by   C. regulator   D. safety

KEY (CORRECT ANSWERS)

1. D	11. B	21. B	31. D
2. C	12. D	22. A	32. A
3. C	13. C	23. B	33. D
4. A	14. D	24. C	34. D
5. D	15. A	25. B	35. A
6. A	16. B	26. C	36. B
7. A	17. A	27. A	37. A
8. C	18. B	28. B	38. C
9. C	19. C	29. C	39. B
10. A	20. B	30. A	40. C

EXAMINATION SECTION
TEST 1

DIRECTIONS: Each question or incomplete statement is followed by several suggested answers or completions. Select the one that BEST answers the question or completes the statement. *PRINT THE LETTER OF THE CORRECT ANSWER IN THE SPACE AT THE RIGHT.*

1. An instrument that is USUALLY mounted on a boiler control panel and which is read in inches of water is known as a(n) _____ gauge.

    A. pressure
    B. draft
    C. stack temperature
    D. Orsat indicator

    1._____

2. The type of pump which SHOULD be used to supply fuel oil to a low pressure boiler is the _____ pump.

    A. centrifugal
    B. diaphragm
    C. rotary gear
    D. reciprocating

    2._____

3. A thermostatic radiator trap which is working satisfactorily will

    A. *open* to pass the steam
    B. *open* to pass the condensate
    C. *close* to retain the cool air
    D. *close* to retain the condensate

    3._____

4. Readings of stack temperature and percentage of carbon dioxide are USEFUL in the boiler room in determining changes in the boiler's _____ efficiency.

    A. mechanical
    B. volumetric
    C. overall
    D. combustion

    4._____

5. In the start-up cycle of a boiler which is equipped with all of the following devices, the device that should be energized BEFORE all the others is the

    A. magnetic oil valve
    B. ignition transformer
    C. gas solenoid valve
    D. fresh air louvre motor

    5._____

6. The one of the following valves which is electrically operated is the _____ valve.

    A. pressure relief
    B. magnetic oil
    C. check
    D. thermostatic control

    6._____

7. In an installation where there is only one fuel oil pump set, a duplex strainer is PREFER-ABLY used because

    A. one side of the strainer can be cleaned without interrupting the flow of oil
    B. one side of the strainer will screen out much finer particles than the other side
    C. the flow of oil can be directed through both sides at the same time, thereby increasing the velocity of the oil
    D. cleaning of a duplex strainer is not required during the heating season

    7._____

8. A higher-than-normal vacuum reading on a gauge which is attached to the suction side of a fuel oil pump GENERALLY indicates that there is

    8._____

A. no oil in the tank
B. a clogged strainer in the suction line
C. a broken fitting in the suction line
D. worn packing on the pump

9. The one of the following which is NOT a possible point of entry of water leaking into the fuel oil storage tank is the

A. fuel fill pipe can
B. sounding well plug
C. steam coil in a fuel oil heater
D. fire box side of the furnace wall

9.___

10. When an air vaporstat which is connected to an automatic rotary cup oil burner senses the loss of primary air pressure in the fan housing, it DE-ENERGIZES the

A. burner motor-starter coil
B. magnetic oil valve
C. secondary air damper control
D. modutrol motor

10.___

11. A steam boiler which is externally fired and in which the hot gases pass through the tubes is COMMONLY known as a _____ boiler.

A. scotch
B. locomotive
C. horizontal return tubular
D. vertical tubular

11.___

12. The modulating pressuretrol on an automatic rotary cup oil-fired boiler controls the

A. modutrol motor circuit
C. burner motor starter
B. magnetic oil valve
D. electric heater

12.___

13. The reason for *blowing down* a boiler is to

A. lower the boiler water level below the boiler tubes
B. reduce the concentration of dissolved solids in the boiler water
C. reduce the concentration of dissolved oxygen in the boiler water
D. eliminate the need for treating the boiler water chemically

13.___

14. The one of the following boiler pressure-actuated devices which should be adjusted to operate at the HIGHEST pressure setting is the

A. pop-safety valve
C. modulating pressuretrol
B. manual-reset pressuretrol
D. limit pressuretrol

14.___

15. The BEST procedure for testing the operation of a low-water cutout is to lower the _____ until the burner shuts off.

A. boiler water level rapidly
B. boiler water level slowly
C. water level in the water column rapidly
D. water level in the water column slowly

15.___

16. If the water disappears from the gauge glass on a low-pressure oil-fired boiler, the FIRST   16.____
action the boiler operator should take is to

    A.   shut off the water
    B.   add water to the boiler until the glass fills up to the correct level
    C.   open the bottom blow-down valve
    D.   blow down the water column

17. On a certain day, the lowest outside temperature was 20°F and the highest was 40°F.   17.____
The number of degree days for this day is

    A. 25   B. 30   C. 35   D. 45

18. A vacuum return line pump should NOT be operated with the electrical control set for   18.____

    A.   continuous operation
    B.   float and vacuum control
    C.   float control *only*
    D.   vacuum control *only*

19. The PREFERRED location for a Dunham Selector is on the _____ exposure of the   19.____
building.

    A.   north   B.   east   C.   south   D.   west

20. Maintaining a Dunham heat balancer in good working order requires annual cleaning of   20.____
its

    A.   radiator fins   B.   relay contacts
    C.   solenoid valve   D.   fulcrum

21. An automatic device used for regulating air temperature is a(n)   21.____

    A.   rheostat   B.   aquastat   C.   thermostat   D.   duostat

22. Smoke alarms which must be installed on oil-fired boilers should create a loud signal and   22.____
a red flashing light upon the emission of an air contaminant whose density, when compared to the standard smoke chart, appears DARKER than Number _____ on the
chart.

    A. 1   B. 2   C. 3   D. 4

23. Samples for the testing of boiler water should be taken from the   23.____

    A.   bottom blow-off   B.   condensate tank
    C.   water column   D.   condensate return line

24. In a building which is heated by an oil-fired boiler, 2,100 gallons of fuel oil were burned in   24.____
a period in which the degree days reached a total of 1,400.
If all other conditions remained constant, the number of gallons of fuel oil that would be
burned in this building during a period in which the degree days reached a total of
3,600 is

    A. 2,400   B. 2,900   C. 4,800   D. 5,400

25. Of the following fuels, the one with the HIGHEST viscosity is

    A. kerosene   B. natural gas
    C. #6 oil   D. #2 oil

25.___

KEY (CORRECT ANSWERS)

1.	B	11.	C
2.	C	12.	A
3.	B	13.	B
4.	D	14.	A
5.	D	15.	B
6.	B	16.	C
7.	A	17.	C
8.	B	18.	D
9.	D	19.	A
10.	B	20.	A

21.	C
22.	A
23.	C
24.	D
25.	C

TEST 2

DIRECTIONS: Each question or incomplete statement is followed by several suggested answers or completions. Select the one that BEST answers the question or completes the statement. *PRINT THE LETTER OF THE CORRECT ANSWER IN THE SPACE AT THE RIGHT.*

1. An indicator card from a steam engine is MOST useful in

    A. determining the boiler pressure
    B. determining the engine speed
    C. adjusting the valve setting
    D. computing the mechanical efficiency

1.____

2. Which of the following statements is MOST NEARLY correct?

    A. A water tube boiler has the combustion gases inside the tubes.
    B. A scotch marine boiler has 2 drums.
    C. A brick set HRT boiler usually has a steel fire box.
    D. The circulation in a boiler may be either gravity or forced.

2.____

3. When the load on a mechanical stoker fired boiler plant furnishing steam for slide valve engine generators drops by 30%, the

    A. stoker should be shut down
    B. fan should be speeded up and the stoker slowed
    C. stoker should be speeded up and the air supply reduced
    D. stoker speed and air supply should be adjusted by reducing both

3.____

4. Which of the following statements is MOST NEARLY correct?

    A. All types of mechanical stokers may be used with equal efficiency under all types of boilers.
    B. Most stokers are designed with a weak member.
    C. The best type of stoker to use is not dependent upon the type of fuel available.
    D. The advisability of installing stokers is not dependent upon the load.

4.____

5. The number and size of safety valves required on a high pressure boiler is dependent upon the

    A. size of the boiler drums
    B. amount of heating surface
    C. number of pounds of fuel burned per square foot of grate per hour
    D. size of the steam main

5.____

6. In changing over a boiler from high pressure (150 lbs. per square inch) to 10 lbs. per square inch, it is usually NECESSARY to

    A. *increase* the size of the safety valves
    B. *decrease* the grate area
    C. *increase* the size of the feed water piping
    D. *increase* the size of the blow down piping

6.____

7. A boiler feed injector becomes temporarily steam bound. To correct this condition, the MOST proper action to take is to

    A. increase boiler pressure
    B. reduce suction lift
    C. wrap it with cold rags
    D. bank fire

7.__

8. The PROPER method of laying up a steam boiler for a period of less than one month is to

    A. drain all the water and let the boiler dry out
    B. fill it with treated water to the top of the tubes
    C. fill it with treated water to the stop valve
    D. fill it with treated water to the level of the upper try cock

8.__

9. In the winter time, heating complaints by tenants should be investigated

    A. only if there are several complaints from one building
    B. only if the outside temperature is below 40°F
    C. immediately
    D. by the assistant superintendent

9.__

10. Compared to the input of the electric ignition transformer associated with #6 oil burners, the output is _____ voltage, _____ current.

    A. higher; higher   B. higher; lower
    C. lower; higher   D. lower; lower

10.__

11. A pressure regulator valve in a compressed air line should be

    A. preceded by a water and oil separator
    B. preceded by a solenoid valve
    C. followed by a water and oil separator
    D. followed by a solenoid valve

11.__

12. A preventive maintenance program in a boiler room should provide for the routine periodic replacement of

    A. badly leaking boiler tubes
    B. electric motors
    C. safety valve springs
    D. programmer electronic tubes

12.__

13. Steam heated hot water tank coils can be tested for leaks by

    A. chemically testing the domestic hot water leaving the tank
    B. chemically testing the condensate leaving the coil
    C. pressure testing the domestic water in the tank
    D. pressure testing the condensate return

13.__

14. The chemical which is added to boiler water to reduce its oxygen content is sodium

    A. carbonate   B. chloride   C. alginate   D. sulphite

14.__

15. Wear in the sleeve bearings of an electric motor is MOST likely to result in a change in the   15.____

    A. pole spacing   B. armature balance
    C. air gap   D. line frequency

16. Assume that only the first few coils of a hot water convector used for heating a room are hot.   16.____
To correct this, you should FIRST

    A. increase the water pressure
    B. increase the water temperature
    C. bleed the air out of the convector
    D. clean the convector pipes

17. When priming occurs in a boiler,   17.____

    A. the fire will be extinguished
    B. the steam becomes superheated and too dry
    C. the fire tubes become overheated and may crack
    D. water particles are carried over with the steam into the steam lines

18. One of the ways to prevent or reduce the amount of smoke from a furnace is to   18.____

    A. reduce the quantity of air supplied to the fire box
    B. supply coal in large quantities and no more than twice a day
    C. cool the fire bed to prevent high temperatures in the fire box
    D. keep live coals at the top of the fire bed

19. Of the following, the SMALLEST size coal is   19.____

    A. chestnut   B. egg   C. buckwheat   D. pea

20. If coal is to be stored, the following precaution should be followed: 20.____

    A. Coal should be piled in conical piles rather than horizontal layers
    B. Coal should be placed in storage on hot summer days
    C. Avoid alternate wetting and drying of coal
    D. Coal should be piled no more than three feet deep

21. The HRT boiler contains   21.____

    A. fire tubes in which hot gases flow
    B. water tubes in which water flows to form steam
    C. no horizontal return tubes
    D. no way in which a vacuum return can be connected

22. A room is properly heated in the winter time when the temperature is about _____ °F and the relative humidity is _____%.   22.____

    A. 70; 40 to 60   B. 78; 40 to 60
    C. 65; 30   D. 75; 90

23. The average temperature on a day in January is 30°F. This would be called a _____ degree day.

    A. 40   B. 35   C. 30   D. 25

23.__

24. The term BTU is used in connection with

    A. heating quality of a fuel
    B. the size of boiler tubes
    C. radiator fittings
    D. heating qualities of radiators

24.__

25. Which one of the following is NOT the cause of clinker formation?

    A. Poor quality coal
    B. Thick fires
    C. Closed ashpit doors
    D. Water sprayed into the ashpit at intervals during the day

25.__

KEY (CORRECT ANSWERS)

1.	C		11.	A
2.	D		12.	D
3.	D		13.	B
4.	B		14.	D
5.	B		15.	C
6.	A		16.	C
7.	C		17.	D
8.	C		18.	D
9.	C		19.	C
10.	B		20.	C

21.	A
22.	A
23.	B
24.	A
25.	D

TEST 3

DIRECTIONS: Each question or incomplete statement is followed by several suggested answers or completions. Select the one that BEST answers the question or completes the statement. *PRINT THE LETTER OF THE CORRECT ANSWER IN THE SPACE AT THE RIGHT.*

1. With steam at a temperature of 365°F in a boiler, which of the following stack gas temperatures would you consider to be good usual operating practice in a plant without economizers, air preheaters, and the like?   1.____

   A. 300°F   B. 500°F   C. 700°F   D. 900°F

2. The percentage of CO_2 in the stack gases is an indication of the   2.____

   A. rate of combustion in the furnace
   B. rate at which excess air is supplied to the furnace
   C. rate of carbon monoxide production in the furnace
   D. temperature of combustion

3. In the most usual type of large capacity oil burner using #6 oil, under *fully automatic* control, the atomization of the oil is produced MAINLY by the   3.____

   A. pressure from the pump
   B. pressure from the secondary air fan
   C. oil temperature from the heater
   D. rotation of the burner assembly by the motor

4. Of the following, the figure which comes the CLOSEST to indicating the number of degree days in a normal heating season in New York City is   4.____

   A. 3000   B. 4000   C. 5000   D. 6000

5. In which of the following methods of steam generation would you expect to obtain reasonably continuous values of CO_2 CLOSEST to the perfect CO_2 value?   5.____
   Automatic

   A. stoker firing with temperature recorder
   B. stoker firing with *hold five timer*
   C. oil firing with *stack switch*
   D. oil firing with *haze regulator*

6. The loss of heat in stack gases for heavy fuel oil is   6.____
   HIGHEST when the CO_2 content is _____% and the stack temperature is _____°

   A. 12; 500   B. 8; 600   C. 6; 700   D. 14; 600

7. A badly sooted HRT boiler under coal firing will show a _____ than a clean boiler.   7.____

   A. higher CO_2 value
   B. lower CO_2 value
   C. higher stack temperature
   D. lower draft loss

8. A unit heater condensing 50 lbs. of low pressure steam per hour would be rated MOST NEARLY at _____ square feet E.D.R.

    A. 50   B. 100   C. 150   D. 200

8.__

9. One horsepower MOST NEARLY equals

    A. 550 ft.-lbs. per second
    B. 3300 ft.-lbs. per minute
    C. 55000 ft.-lbs. per hour
    D. 10000 ft.-lbs. per minute

9.__

10. A pressure gauge attached to a standpipe system shows a pressure of 36 pounds per square inch.
The head of water, in feet, above the gauge is MOST NEARLY

    A. 24   B. 36   C. 60   D. 83

10.__

11. Of the following, the term *vapor barrier* would MOST likely be associated with

    A. electric service installation
    B. insulation materials
    C. fuel oil tank installation
    D. domestic gas piping

11.__

12. Pitot tubes are used to

    A. test feed water for impurities
    B. measure air or gas flow in a duct
    C. prevent overheating of elements of a steam gauge
    D. control the ignition system of an oil burner

12.__

13. In warm air heating and in ventilating systems, laboratories and kitchens should NOT be equipped with return ducts in order to

    A. keep air velocities in other returns as high as possible
    B. reduce fire hazards
    C. reduce the possibility of circulating odors through the system
    D. keep the temperature high in these rooms

13.__

14. One square foot of equivalent direct steam radiation (EDR) is equivalent to a heat emission of _____ BTU per _____.

    A. 150; hour   B. 240; minute
    C. 150; minute   D. 240; hour

14.__

15. Of the following, the one which is LEAST likely to cause continuous vibration of an operating motor is

    A. a faulty starting circuit
    B. excessive belt tension
    C. the misalignment of motor and driven equipment
    D. loose bearings

15.__

16. The function of a steam trap is to   16.____

    A. remove sediment and dirt from steam
    B. remove air and non-condensible gases from steam
    C. relieve excessive steam pressure to the atmosphere
    D. remove condensate from a pipe or an apparatus

17. The temperature at which air is just saturated with the moisture present in it is called its   17.____

    A. relative humidity   B. absolute humidity
    C. humid temperature   D. dew point

18. Of the following, the one which is NOT a general class of oil burners is the _____ atom-   18.____
izing.

    A. water   B. rotary cup
    C. mechanical   D. air

19. Of the following, the one which should be between a boiler and its safety valve is   19.____

    A. a swing check valve of a size larger than that of the safety valve
    B. a butterfly valve located in the boiler nozzle
    C. a gate valve of the same nominal size as that of the safety valve
    D. no valve of any type

20. The term *spinner cup* refers to   20.____

    A. screw-type stokers   B. gun-type oil burners
    C. rotary-type oil burners   D. chain grate stokers

21. A gun-type burner is often used on a   21.____

    A. pot-type oil burner
    B. low pressure gas boiler
    C. coal underfeed stoker boiler
    D. high pressure oil-fired boiler

22. Of the following, the action that should be taken as the FIRST step if a properly adjusted   22.____
safety valve on a steam boiler *pops off* when in operation is

    A. open the draft
    B. add more water to the boiler
    C. wire the valve shut
    D. reduce the draft

23. When the water gets below the safe level in an operating boiler, it is BEST to   23.____

    A. add new water up to the safe level and open up the fire so that the water will heat
        quickly
    B. check the fire and let the boiler cool down before new water is added
    C. add new water to the boiler immediately
    D. check the fire and empty the boiler

24. Vents on fuel oil storage tanks are used to 24.___

   A. fill the fuel tanks
   B. allow air to escape during filling
   C. check oil flash points
   D. make tank fuel soundings

25. Of the following, the MOST desirable way to remove carbon deposits from the atomizing 25.___
   cup of an oil burner is to

   A. apply a hot flame to the carbonized surfaces to burn off the carbon deposits
   B. use kerosene to loosen the deposits and wipe with a soft cloth
   C. wash the cup with a mild trisodium phosphate solution and dry with a cloth
   D. use a scraper, followed by light rubbing with emery cloth

---

KEY (CORRECT ANSWERS)

1.	B		11.	B
2.	B		12.	B
3.	D		13.	C
4.	C		14.	D
5.	D		15.	A
6.	C		16.	D
7.	C		17.	D
8.	D		18.	A
9.	A		19.	D
10.	D		20.	C

21.	D
22.	D
23.	B
24.	B
25.	B

EXAMINATION SECTION
TEST 1

DIRECTIONS: Each question or incomplete statement is followed by several suggested answers or completions. Select the one that BEST answers the question or completes the statement. *PRINT THE LETTER OF THE CORRECT ANSWER IN THE SPACE AT THE RIGHT.*

1. The flow of oil in an automatic rotary cup oil burner is regulated by a(n)   1.____

    A. thermostat   B. metering valve
    C. pressure relief valve   D. electric eye

2. The type of fuel which must be *pre-heated* before it can be burned efficiently is   2.____

    A. natural gas   B. pea coal
    C. Number 2 oil   D. Number 6 oil

3. A suction gauge in a fuel-oil transfer system is USUALLY located   3.____

    A. *before* the strainer
    B. *after* the strainer and *before* the pump
    C. *after* the pump and *before* the pressure relief valve
    D. *after* the pressure relief valve

4. The FIRST item that should be checked before starting the fire in a steam boiler is the   4.____

    A. thermostat   B. vacuum pump
    C. boiler water level   D. steam pressure

5. Operation of a boiler that has been *sealed* by the department of buildings is   5.____

    A. prohibited
    B. permitted when the outside temperature is below 32°F
    C. permitted between the hours of 6:00 A.M. and 8:00 A.M. and 9:00 P.M. and 11:00 P.M.
    D. permitted only for the purposes of heating domestic water

6. Lowering the thermostat setting by 5 degrees during the heating season will result in a fuel saving of MOST NEARLY _____ percent.   6.____

    A. 2   B. 5   C. 20   D. 50

7. An electrically-driven rotary fuel oil pump must be protected from internal damage by the installation in the oil line of a   7.____

    A. discharge-side strainer   B. check valve
    C. suction gauge   D. pressure relief valve

8. Baffle plates are sometimes put into furnaces to   8.____

    A. change the direction of heated gases
    B. increase the combustion of the fuel
    C. retard the burning of the gases
    D. prevent overloading of the combustion chamber

9. An operating boiler explosion may be caused by 9.__

    A. accumulation of gas in the furnace
    B. too deep a fire
    C. overpressure of steam
    D. too much water in the boiler

10. Of the following, the MOST important precaution that should be taken when *cutting in* a boiler in a battery is to see that the 10.__

    A. water column is at least 1 inch below top row of tubes
    B. non-return valve is closed when the boiler pressure is rising
    C. safety valves function properly
    D. boiler pressure is about equal to header pressure

11. A condensate feedwater tank in a low pressure steam plant 11.__

    A. is hermetically sealed to prevent contamination of feedwater
    B. contains a surface blow down line
    C. is vented to the atmosphere
    D. has a vacuum breaker exposed to the atmosphere

12. Of the following, the FIRST action to take in the event a low pressure steam boiler gauge glass breaks is to 12.__

    A. bank the fires
    B. close the water gauge glass cocks
    C. open the safety valve
    D. blow down the boiler

13. A *barometric damper* would be used in a boiler installation fired under draft conditions that are called 13.__

    A. induced   B. natural
    C. regenerate   D. forced

14. The flue gas temperature, when firing oil, should be just high enough to evaporate any contained moisture in order to 14.__

    A. prevent an acid from forming and eroding the breeching
    B. decrease the amount of excess air needed
    C. prevent an air pollution condition
    D. lower the combustion efficiency of the boiler

15. A compound gauge in a boiler room 15.__

    A. measures pressures above and below atmospheric pressure
    B. indicates the degree of compounding in a steam engine
    C. shows the quantity of boiler treatment compound on hand
    D. measures steam and water pressure

16. In the combustion of the common fuels, the PRINCIPAL boiler heat loss is that due to the heat   16.____

    A. carried away by the moisture in the fuel
    B. lost by radiation
    C. carried away by the Hue gases
    D. lost by incomplete combustion

17. Of the following, the CORRECT sequence of steps to use when removing a boiler from service in order to perform extensive repairs on it is   17.____

    A. discontinue firing, drain boiler, turn off valves, and cool boiler
    B. discontinue firing, drain boiler, and turn off valves
    C. turn off valves, drain boiler, discontinue firing, and cool boiler
    D. discontinue firing, turn off valves, cool boiler, and drain boiler

18. The one of the following conditions that will MOST likely cause fuel oil pressure to fluctu-ate is   18.____

    A. a faulty pressure gauge
    B. a clean oil strainer
    C. cold oil in the suction line
    D. an overtight pump drive belt

19. The cooler in a Freon 12 refrigeration system that is equipped with automatic protective devices is MOST likely to be accidentally damaged by water freeze-up when the sys-tem('s)   19.____

    A. is operating at reduced load
    B. is operating at rated load
    C. condenser water flow is interrupted
    D. is being pumped down

20. The capacity of a water-cooled condenser is LEAST affected by the   20.____

    A. water temperature
    B. refrigerant temperature
    C. surrounding air temperature
    D. quantity of condenser water being circulated

21. Of the following chemicals used in boiler feedwater treatment, the one that should be used to RETARD corrosion in the boiler circuit due to dissolved oxygen is sodium   21.____

    A. aluminate   B. carbonate   C. phosphate   D. sulfite

22. The heating system in a certain school is equipped with vacuum return condensate pumps.
The MOST likely place for an air-vent valve to be installed in this plant is on   22.____

    A. each radiator
    B. the outlet of the domestic hot water steam heating coil
    C. the pressure side of the vacuum pump
    D. the shell of the domestic hot water tank

23. *Priming* of a steam boiler is NOT caused by

    A. load swings
    B. uneven fire distribution
    C. too high a water level
    D. high alkalinity of the boiler water

23.___

24. A Hartford loop is used in school heating systems PRIMARILY to

    A. provide for thermal expansion of the steam distribution piping
    B. equalize the water level in two or more boilers
    C. prevent siphoning of water out of the boiler
    D. by-pass the electric fuel oil heaters when the steam heaters are operating

24.___

25. Of the following, the MOST likely use for temperature-indicating crayons by a custodian-engineer is in

    A. checking the operation of the radiator traps
    B. replacing room thermometers that have been vandalized
    C. indicating possible sources of spontaneous combustion
    D. checking the effectiveness of an insulating panel

25.___

KEY (CORRECT ANSWERS)

1. B		11. C	
2. D		12. B	
3. B		13. B	
4. C		14. A	
5. A		15. A	
6. C		16. C	
7. D		17. D	
8. A		18. C	
9. C		19. D	
10. D		20. C	

21. D
22. B
23. D
24. C
25. A

TEST 2

DIRECTIONS: Each question or incomplete statement is followed by several suggested answers or completions. Select the one that BEST answers the question or completes the statement. *PRINT THE LETTER OF THE CORRECT ANSWER IN THE SPACE AT THE RIGHT.*

1. A boiler horsepower is defined as the evaporation of _____ lbs. of water per hour from and at 212°F.

   A.   32.0   B.   14.7   C.   34.5   D.   29.9

   1.____

2. The steam drum of a water tube boiler is 16 feet long and 42 inches in diameter. Assuming that the normal water line is at the drum center-line, the water content of the drum under normal operating conditions is MOST NEARLY

   A.   700 gallons   B.   600 gallons
   C.   400 gallons   D.   400 cubic feet

   2.____

3. In selecting a coal from its *proximate analysis,* which of the following coals would you consider to be BEST suited for use in a boiler plant in a heavily populated city? _____ ash - _____ volatile matter.

   A.   7%; 18%   B.   10%; 21%   C.   12%; 17%   D.   5%; 25%

   3.____

4. Which of the following type of grates should be used for ease in cleaning fires, when hand-firing large boilers with #1 buckwheat, under natural draft at heavy loads?

   A.   Dumping grates
   B.   Stationary grates with 3/4" air spaces
   C.   Stationary grates (pinhole type)
   D.   Shaking grates

   4.____

5. Which of the following fuels contains the GREATEST number of heat units per pound?

   A.   Hard coal   B.   No. 6 fuel oil
   C.   Yard screenings   D.   Bituminous coal

   5.____

6. In the usual water tube boiler plant using coal under natural draft, the point where the MAXIMUM negative draft gage reading may be obtained is

   A.   at the top of the stack   B.   at the base of the stack
   C.   over the fire   D.   in the last pass

   6.____

7. The purpose of admitting air over the fire in a coal-fired furnace is USUALLY to

   A.   reduce the stack gas temperature
   B.   improve the draft
   C.   reduce the smoke
   D.   reduce the draft

   7.____

8. If the volume of air in cubic feet per minute for combustion is represented by X, which of the following values of X would MOST NEARLY represent the Cfm of stack gas, under usual conditions, that an induced draft fan would have to handle?

   A.   X   B.   2X   C.   3X   D.   4X

   8.____

9. If the stack switch of an oil burner becomes excessively sooted, a condition MOST likely to result is   9.___

    A. continuous shutting down of the burner shortly after it starts up
    B. excessive flow of oil to the burner resulting in a smoky fire
    C. excessive fire due to failure to cut off current to the burner motor
    D. failure of the warp switch of the relay to operate

10. Suppose that a small oil fire has broken out in the boiler, room in your building. Under these circumstances, the extinguisher LEAST suitable for use is   10.___

    A. soda-acid   B. pyrene
    C. foamite   D. carbon dioxide

11. Of the following, a low *power factor* would MOST likely result from   11.___

    A. Corlis valve engine operating at less than half normal rated load
    B. a large DC motor operating at 20% below normal speed
    C. a large induction motor operating at 60% normal rated capacity
    D. a storage battery on which the voltage has dropped to 10% below normal

12. A heating plant is to be laid up for the summer.
With respect to fire surfaces, the PROPER procedure after cleaning is to   12.___

    A. keep them moist with water applied with a spray
    B. paint them with a good plastic paint
    C. coat them with oil
    D. paint them with a metallic paint

13. When starting a fire in the boiler, the custodian should   13.___

    A. have ashpit doors and dampers closed before firing to give proper draft
    B. place about one inch of coal directly on the grate and then ignite with oil waste placed on top of the coal
    C. keep dampers closed and ashpit doors open to obtain proper drafts
    D. spread a bed of coal about three inches thick on the grates and then build fire on this bed

14. The vacuum system of storm heating does NOT have   14.___

    A. air valves on radiators
    B. thermostatic traps on radiators
    C. drip traps
    D. steam risers connected to radiators

15. The capacity of a heating boiler is USUALLY expressed in terms of   15.___

    A. square feet of radiation
    B. cubic feet of steam
    C. pounds of steam per hour
    D. the number of radiators required

16. The hammering noise in a heating system is caused by   16.____

    A.   the pressure of water acting against the walls of the water pipe supplying the boiler
    B.   contact of steam and water in the radiators
    C.   the vibration of loose fire tubes in the boiler
    D.   the vacuum effect of the release of water in the steam gauge

17. In one hour, one square foot of grate for a tubular boiler will burn, with natural draft, about   17.____
_____ lbs. of hard coal.

    A. 12   B. 25   C. 6   D. 30

18. The velocity of air in a ventilation duct is USUALLY measured with a(n)   18.____

    A.   hydrometer   B.   psychrometer
    C.   pyrometer   D.   pitot tube

19. The device which starts and stops the flow of oil into an automatic rotary cup oil burner is   19.____
USUALLY called a(n) _____ valve.

    A.   magnetic oil   B.   oil metering
    C.   oil check   D.   relief

20. A vacuum breaker, used on a steam heated domestic hot water tank, is USUALLY con-   20.____
nected to the

    A.   circulating pump   B.   tank wall
    C.   aquastat   D.   steam coil flange

21. A vacuum pump in a low pressure steam heating system which is equipped with a float   21.____
switch, a vacuum switch, a magnetic starter, and a selector switch can be operated on

    A.   float, vacuum, or automatic
    B.   float, vacuum, or continuous
    C.   vacuum, automatic, or continuous
    D.   float, automatic, or continuous

22. If the temperature of the condensate returning to the vacuum pump in a low pressure   22.____
steam vacuum heating system is above 180°F, the trouble may be caused by

    A.   faulty radiator traps
    B.   room thermostats being set too high
    C.   uninsulated return lines
    D.   too many radiators being shut off

23. A feedwater regulator operates to   23.____

    A.   shut down the burner when the water is low
    B.   maintain the water in the boiler at a predetermined level
    C.   drain the water from the boiler
    D.   regulate the temperature of the feedwater

24. An automatically fired steam boiler is equipped with an automatic low water cut-off.   24.____
The low water cut-off is USUALLY actuated by

    A.   steam pressure   B.   fuel pressure
    C.   float action   D.   water temperature

25. Low pressure steam or an electric heater is USUALLY required for heating # _____ fuel 25.___
oil.

    A. 1   B. 2   C. 4   D. 6

KEY (CORRECT ANSWERS)

1.	C		11.	C
2.	B		12.	C
3.	A		13.	D
4.	A		14.	A
5.	B		15.	A
6.	B		16.	B
7.	C		17.	A
8.	B		18.	D
9.	A		19.	A
10.	A		20.	D

21.	D
22.	A
23.	B
24.	C
25.	D

TEST 3

DIRECTIONS: Each question or incomplete statement is followed by several suggested answers or completions. Select the one that BEST answers the question or completes the statement. *PRINT THE LETTER OF THE CORRECT ANSWER IN THE SPACE AT THE RIGHT.*

1. An unusually high vacuum reading in a fuel oil suction line may indicate that the   1._____

    A. level in the fuel oil tank is low
    B. oil preheater is leaking
    C. oil strainer is dirty
    D. oil is too hot

2. The MAIN reason for modulating the flame in a steam heating boiler that has an automatic rotary cup oil burner is to   2._____

    A. reduce the number of start and stop operations
    B. guarantee a high-fire start
    C. vary the cut-out pressure
    D. vary the cut-in pressure

3. The device on a rotary cup oil burner which senses primary air failure is the   3._____

    A. draft sensing device   B. aquastat
    C. draft alarm   D. vaporstat

4. A 10,000 gallon pressurized house tank contains 8030 gallons of water, and the pressure gauge reads 60 psi.   4._____
In the event of a power failure, the number of gallons of water which can be drawn out of the tank before the pressure reading drops to 50 psi is MOST NEARLY

    A. 300   B. 2000   C. 6000   D. 8000

5. The heat balancer in a Dunham steam heating system   5._____

    A. measures indoor temperatures
    B. controls the firing rate of two or more boilers
    C. measures outdoor temperatures
    D. reacts to the rate of heat output

6. In a sub-atmospheric steam heating system, the steam temperature corresponding to a vacuum of 15 inches of mercury is MOST NEARLY _____ °F.   6._____

    A. 180   B. 200   C. 212   D. 218

7. When the fuel supply to a rotary cup oil burner is cut off, the burner motor switch should open within _____ seconds.   7._____

    A. 2   B. 4 to 8   C. 12 to 18   D. 30 to 40

8. Which of the following is USUALLY used in the construction of a steam pressure gauge?   8._____

    A. Perfect circle tube   B. Venturi tube
    C. Bourdon tube   D. Elastic linkage

9. Usually when a large room is gradually filled with people, the room temperature   9._

    A. and humidity both decrease
    B. increases and the humidity decreases
    C. and humidity increase
    D. decreases and the humidity increases

10. A foot valve at the intake end of the suction line of a pump serves MAINLY to   10._

    A. maintain pump prime
    B. filter out large particles in the fluid
    C. increase the maximum suction lift of the pump
    D. increase pump flow rate

11. BEST combustion conditions exist when the stack haze as indicated on the Ringelman   11._
chart scale is Number

    A. 1   B. 3   C. 5   D. 6

12. A pop safety valve is COMMONLY a   12._

    A. member with a rupture section
    B. dead weight valve
    C. ball and lever valve
    D. spring loaded valve

13. Fusible plugs used as protective devices in HRT boilers producing low pressure steam   13.__
should melt at temperatures

    A. above the temperature of the steam and below the temperature of the flue gases
    B. at the same temperature as the steam
    C. above the usual temperature of both the flue gases and the steam
    D. at about the same temperature as the flue gases

14. The high low water alarm of a steam boiler is USUALLY located in the   14.__

    A. boiler   B. gauge glass
    C. water column   D. feedwater

15. What is an ADVANTAGE of shaking grates over stationary grates?   15.__

    A. The fire can be cleaned without opening the fire door.
    B. They are warp-proof.
    C. They are usually more sturdily constructed than stationary grates.
    D. Deeper firebed can usually be maintained.

16. An ACCEPTABLE method of detecting air leaks in the setting of a boiler is   16.___

    A. placing an open flame or burning torch near the point where the leaks are suspected
    B. coating the suspected parts of the setting with heavy grease
    C. coating the suspected points of leakage with a heavy soap emulsion
    D. inspecting suspected areas of leakage with a powerful light and hand magnifier

17. To avoid injury to an oil supply pump in the event of a stoppage in the discharge line, there should be provided a _____ line.

    A. pressure regulating valve in the suction
    B. pressure relief valve in the discharge
    C. viscosity valve in the suction
    D. check valve in the discharge

17.____

18. At which of the following locations should you find a remote control switch?

    A. In principal's office   B. In engineer's office
    C. At boiler room entrance   D. At entrance to building

18.____

19. Sprinkler systems are more often found in the following location:

    A. Boiler room   B. Gym
    C. Storage rooms   D. Science rooms

19.____

20. If a gas range flame is all whitish yellow, what does it indicate?

    A. Insufficient gas pressure
    B. Insufficient air
    C. Not enough gas
    D. Too much air

20.____

21. If glass on water column breaks when boiler is operating, you should

    A. bank fire   B. shut off oil burner
    C. use tri-cocks   D. close main steam valve

21.____

22. The BEST of the following combinations of instruments to use in checking the combustion efficiency of a heating boiler is

    A. anemometer, stack thermometer, and orsat apparatus
    B. draft gage, psychrometer, and barometer
    C. draft gage, stack thermometer, and orsat apparatus
    D. draft gage, stack thermometer, and barometer

22.____

23. The one of the following that does NOT indicate low water in a steam boiler is the

    A. fusible plug   B. safety valve
    C. tri-cocks   D. gauge glass

23.____

24. The increase in the stack temperature toward the end of the heating season above what it was at the beginning of the season is an indication that the

    A. radiators and convectors are air bound
    B. tubes and heating surfaces of the boiler are becoming insulated with soot
    C. furnace fire brick is failing
    D. heat content of the fuel is improving

24.____

25. The color of fire lines is

    A. yellow   B. green   C. brown   D. red

25.____

KEY (CORRECT ANSWERS)

1.	C	11.	A
2.	A	12.	D
3.	D	13.	B
4.	A	14.	C
5.	D	15.	A
6.	A	16.	A
7.	B	17.	B
8.	C	18.	C
9.	C	19.	C
10.	A	20.	D

21.	C
22.	C
23.	B
24.	B
25.	D

———

EXAMINATION SECTION
TEST 1

DIRECTIONS: Each question or incomplete statement is followed by several suggested answers or completions. Select the one that BEST answers the question or completes the statement. *PRINT THE LETTER OF THE CORBECT ANSWER IN THE SPACE AT THE RIGHT.*

1. In high pressure electric generating plants in large buildings, heating the feedwater from 70° F to 180° F with exhaust steam usually will DECREASE the fuel consumption by

   A. 5%   B. 10%   C. 15%   D. 20%

   1.____

2. The direct room radiator with a pneumatically controlled steam heating system is cold, while the adjoining rooms are heated adequately.
   Of the following, the FIRST thing you would check in the room is the

   A. steam pipe in the room before the pneumatic steam valve
   B. thermostat
   C. pneumatic steam valve
   D. thermostatic trap

   2.____

3. The USUAL vacuum gage on a steam heating system reads in

   A. inches of vacuum   B. feet of mercury
   C. inches of water   D. feet of water

   3.____

4. In a mechanical pressure type burner using #6 oil heated to 230° F by steam, the oil is atomized by

   A. centrifugal force   B. steam temperature
   C. oil temperature   D. oil pressure

   4.____

5. A vaporstat with separate motor driven oil pump used on a fully automatic heavy oil burning rotary cup installation is GENERALLY used to

   A. keep the boiler pressure within proper limits
   B. regulate the pressure of the primary air
   C. regulate the pressure of the secondary air
   D. shut down the burner when primary air failure occurs

   5.____

6. In estimating the amount of work being done by a steam driven water pump, the one of the following items which is usually the MOST important in the calculation of pump horsepower is the

   A. temperature of the water
   B. suction lift
   C. steam pressure
   D. gallons pumped

   6.____

7. The term *fixture unit* USUALLY refers to

   A. the number of lamp sockets in an electric lighting fixture
   B. the number of fixtures in a room or building

   7.____

C. a rate of flow
D. amperes per second

8. In a hot water heating system, it may be necessary to *bleed* radiators to   8.___

    A. relieve high steam pressure
    B. permit entrapped air to escape
    C. allow condensate to return to the boiler
    D. drain off waste water

9. Which oil would have the GREATEST sulphur content?   9.___

    A. #2   B. #6   C. #1   D. #4

10. A *scrubber* would be MOST commonly found on a   10.___

    A. vacuum pump
    B. snow plow
    C. incinerator
    D. auditorium fresh air blower

11. Combustion efficiency can be determined from an appropriate chart used in conjunction   11.___
with

    A. steam temperature and steam pressure
    B. flue gas temperature and percentage of CO_2
    C. flue gas temperature and fuel heating value
    D. oil temperature and steam pressure

12. One of the possible results of closing ashpit doors to regulate draft is   12.___

    A. warping or melting of grates
    B. reduced formation of clinkers
    C. steam will become superheated
    D. live coals will fall into the ashpit

13. The MOST important reason for blowing down a boiler water column and gauge glass is   13.___
to

    A. prevent the gauge glass level from rising too high
    B. relieve stresses in the gauge glass
    C. insure a true water level reading
    D. insure a true pressure gauge reading

14. The secondary voltage of a transformer used for ignition in a fuel oil burner has a range   14.___
of MOST NEARLY _____ volts.

    A. 120 to 240   B. 440 to 660
    C. 660 to 1,200   D. 5,000 to 15,000

15. Assume that during the month of April there were 3 days with an average outdoor tem-   15.___
perature of 30° F, 7 days with 40° F, 10 days with 50° F, 3 days with 60° F, and 7 days with
65°F. The number of degree days for the month was

    A. 330   B. 445   C. 595   D. 1,150

16. The pH of boiler feedwater is USUALLY maintained within the range of   16._____

    A.   4 to 5   B.   6 to 7   C.   10 to 12   D.   13 to 14

17. The admission of steam to the coils of a domestic hot water supply tank is regulated by   17._____
a(n)

    A.   pressure regulating valve
    B.   immersion type temperature gauge
    C.   check valve
    D.   thermostatic control valve

18. The device which senses primary air failure in a rotary cup oil burner is USUALLY called   18._____
a(n)

    A.   vaporstat   B.   anemometer
    C.   venturi   D.   pressure gauge

19. A vacuum pump is used in a(n) _____ heating system.   19._____

    A.   steam   B.   hot air   C.   hot water   D.   electric

20. An expansion tank is used in a(n) _____ heating system.   20._____

    A.   steam   B.   hot air   C.   hot water   D.   electric

21. The thermostat in the office area of a public building should have a winter daytime setting   21._____
of about _____° F.

    A.   50   B.   60   C.   70   D.   80

22. A lazy bar is MOST often associated with   22._____

    A.   radiators   B.   vents   C.   fences   D.   boilers

23. The domestic hot water in a large public building is circulated by   23._____

    A.   gravity flow
    B.   a pump which runs continuously
    C.   a pump which is controlled by water pressure
    D.   a pump which is controlled by water temperature

24. Of the following, the hacksaw blade BEST suited for cutting thin-walled tubing is one   24._____
which has _____ teeth/inch.

    A.   14   B.   18   C.   24   D.   32

25. The emergency switch for a fully automatic oil burner is USUALLY located   25._____

    A.   at the entrance to the boiler room
    B.   on the burner
    C.   at the electrical distribution panel in the boiler room
    D.   at the electric service meter panel

KEY (CORRECT ANSWERS)

1.	B		11.	B
2.	A		12.	A
3.	A		13.	C
4.	D		14.	D
5.	D		15.	B
6.	D		16.	C
7.	C		17.	D
8.	B		18.	A
9.	B		19.	A
10.	C		20.	C

21.	C
22.	D
23.	D
24.	D
25.	A

TEST 2

DIRECTIONS: Each question or incomplete statement is followed by several suggested answers or completions. Select the one that BEST answers the question or completes the statement. *PRINT THE LETTER OF THE CORRECT ANSWER IN THE SPACE AT THE RIGHT.*

1. A compound gauge is calibrated to read   1.____

   A. pressure *only*   B. vacuum *only*
   C. vacuum and pressure   D. temperature and humidity

2. In a mechanical pressure-atomizing type oil burner, the oil is atomized by using an atom-   2.____
   izing tip and

   A. steam pressure   B. pump pressure
   C. compressed air   D. a spinning cup

3. A good over-the-fire draft in a natural draft furnace should be APPROXIMATELY _____   3.____
   inches of water _____ .

   A. 5.0; positive pressure   B. 0.05; positive pressure
   C. 0.05; vacuum   D. 5.0; vacuum

4. When it is necessary to add chemicals to a heating boiler, it should be done   4.____

   A. immediately after boiler blowdown
   B. after the boiler has been cleaned internally of sludge, scale, and other foreign mat-
       ter
   C. at periods when condensate flow to the boiler is small
   D. at a time when there is a heavy flow of condensate to the boiler

5. The modutrol motor on a rotary cup oil burner burning #6 fuel oil automatically operates   5.____
   the primary air damper,

   A. secondary air damper, and oil metering valve
   B. secondary air damper, and magnetic oil valve
   C. oil metering valve, a'nd magnetic oil valve
   D. and magnetic oil valve

6. The manual-reset pressuretrol is classified as a _____ control.   6.____

   A. safety and operating
   B. limit and operating
   C. limit and safety
   D. limit, operating, and safety

7. If you had too much oil, what would you do for good combustion?   7.____

   A. Increase secondary air   B. Increase primary air
   C. Increase both   D. Lower oil pressure

8. *Cascading* of raw city water when filling a cleaned boiler should be avoided because it   8.____

   A. is harmful to the mud drum
   B. adds additional free oxygen in the boiler

C. adds considerable time to the filling procedure
D. will stress tube and sheet joints

9. The average temperature on a day in January was 24° F. The number of degree days for 9.___
that day was

A. 12   B. 24   C. 41   D. 48

10. With the same outdoor winter temperatures, the load on a heating boiler starting up is 10.___
greater than the normal morning load MAINLY because of

A. loss of heat escaping through the stack
B. steam required to heat boiler water and piping to radiators
C. viscosity of the fuel oil
D. low outdoor temperatures

11. The FIRST operation when starting a boiler after it has been on bank overnight should 11.___
be to

A. blow down the boiler
B. clean the furnace
C. check the gate valves
D. look at the water gauge and try the gauge cocks

12. Proper combustion of fuel is obtained when 12.___

A. the flue gases contain a large percentage of carbon monoxide
B. black smoke appears in the flue gases
C. there is 10 to 15 percent carbon dioxide in the flue gases
D. the flame of the fire is high enough to reach the fire tubes

13. The vertical pipes leading from the steam mains to the radiators are called 13.___

A. expansion joints   B. radiant coils
C. drip lines   D. risers

14. Try cocks are used to 14.___

A. determine the exact water level in the boiler
B. find the approximate water level in the boiler
C. learn if steam is being generated in the boiler
D. obtain an approximate idea of the steam pressure

15. If a ton of anthracite coal occupies approximately 40 cubic feet, the space required, in 15.___
cubic yards, for 135 tons of coal is

A. 200   B. 128.6   C. 600   D. 40

16. During the winter heating season, it is BEST practice to blow down the boiler 16.___

A. once a month
B. twice daily
C. only when new grates are installed
D. once a day

17. A boiler blow-off valve is PRIMARILY used to   17.____

    A. maintain constant boiler pressure
    B. drain water from the boiler
    C. allow air to enter boiler when proper temperature is reached
    D. reduce boiler pressure

18. When a room becomes heated above the upper temperature setting of a thermostat   18.____
    which controls a check damper, the damper is

    A. automatically closed to reduce the air supply
    B. opened to admit more air
    C. not affected, but the supply of the boiler is increased
    D. partially closed and the water supply of the boiler is increased

19. The device which protects the boiler from damage due to low water is the   19.____

    A. fusible plug   B. fusible link
    C. vaporstat   D. aquastat

20. In a low-pressure fire-tube boiler, the oil burner should be shut off BEFORE   20.____

    A. operating the soot blower
    B. taking a flue gas sample
    C. blowing down the boiler
    D. blowing down the water column

21. A domestic hot water circulating pump is started and stopped automatically by means of   21.____
    a(n) _____ line.

    A. pressuretrol in the supply
    B. pressuretrol in the return
    C. aquastat in the supply
    D. aquastat in the return

22. On a steam-heated domestic hot water generator, the device which acts to PREVENT   22.____
    damage to the coils due to a high internal pressure differential between the coil and the
    tank is the

    A. pressure relief valve   B. vacuum breaker
    C. air vent valve   D. steam trap

23. In the city, the rules and regulations concerning the cleaning of a water tank which is part   23.____
    of a building's domestic water supply are specified by the

    A. fire department
    B. department of housing and buildings
    C. city sanitary code
    D. board of water supply

24. A housing fireman, making a preliminary inspection of a fuel oil delivery truck, discovers   24.___
    that the level of the oil in one compartment is far below the marker.
    In this case, he SHOULD

    A. reject the shipment and order that it be returned to the terminal
    B. measure the level of the oil in the low compartment by *sticking* and report his find-
       ings to the superintendent before unloading
    C. read the liquidometer gauge before allowing the truck to be unloaded and again
       after it has been unloaded and record the difference in gallons to determine the
       amount for which payment should be made
    D. ignore the low level if it is in only one compartment

25. The *flame eye* or electronic photocell to detect a proper oil flame or flame failure is USU-   25.___
    ALLY mounted in an opening

    A. in the smoke box of the boiler
    B. in the chimney breeching in the direction of the hot gases
    C. on the front of the combustion chamber above the burner
    D. on a side wall of the furnace above the burner center line

_____

KEY (CORRECT ANSWERS)

1.	C	11.	D
2.	B	12.	C
3.	C	13.	D
4.	D	14.	B
5.	A	15.	A
6.	C	16.	D
7.	B	17.	B
8.	B	18.	B
9.	C	19.	A
10.	B	20.	C

21.	D
22.	B
23.	C
24.	B
25.	C

_____

TEST 3

DIRECTIONS: Each question or incomplete statement is followed by several suggested answers or completions. Select the one that BEST answers the question or completes the statement. *PRINT THE LETTER OF THE CORRECT ANSWER IN THE SPACE AT THE RIGHT.*

1. The lowest visible part of the water column attached to an HRT boiler should be AT LEAST   1.____

    A.   3 inches above the top row of tubes
    B.   6 inches above the fusible plug
    C.   1 inch above the top row of tubes
    D.   1/2 inch above the fusible plug

2. The function of a fusible plug is to   2.____

    A.   melt if the water temperature is too high
    B.   prevent too high a furnace temperature
    C.   prevent excessive steam pressure from developing in the boiler
    D.   melt when the water level drops below the level of the plug

3. To control the temperature of water in a domestic water supply tank, the device used is USUALLY a   3.____

    A.   thermostat   B.   pressuretrol
    C.   solenoid valve   D.   aquastat

4. A house trap is a device placed in the house drain immediately inside the foundation wall of the building.   4.____
Its MAIN purpose is to

    A.   trap sediment flowing in the house drain to the street sewer
    B.   prevent sewer gases from circulating in the building plumbing system
    C.   maintain air pressure balance in the vent lines of the plumbing system
    D.   provide a means for cleaning the waste lines of the plumbing system

5. In the care and operation of steam boilers, a procedure that is considered GOOD practice is to   5.____

    A.   open the safety valve in the event low water is found
    B.   refill the boiler with cold water when the boiler is hot
    C.   remove the boiler from service immediately if the water level cannot be determined because the gauge glass is broken
    D.   use hot water where possible in refilling a boiler prior to firing

6. A sequential draft control on a rotary cup oil-fired boiler should operate to   6.____

    A.   *open* the automatic damper at the end of the post-purge period
    B.   *open* the automatic damper when the draft has increased during normal burner operation
    C.   *close* the automatic damper just before the burner motor starts up
    D.   *close* the automatic damper after the burner goes off and the burner cycle is completed

7. The one of the following components of flue gas that indicates, when present, that more excess air is being supplied than is being used is   7.___

    A. carbon dioxide   B. carbon monoxide
    C. nitrogen   D. oxygen

8. An ADVANTAGE that a float-thermostatic steam trap has over a float-type steam trap of comparable rating is that a float-thermostatic trap   8.___

    A. requires less maintenance
    B. is easier to install
    C. allows non-condensable gases to escape
    D. releases the condensate at a higher temperature

9. A pump delivers 165 pounds of water per minute against a total head of 100 feet. The water horsepower of this pump is _____ HP.   9.___

    A. 1/2   B. 2   C. 5   D. 20

10. Of the following, the BEST instrument to use to measure over-the-fire draft is the   10.___

    A. Bourdon tube gauge   B. inclined manometer
    C. mercury manometer   D. potentiometer

11. The temperature of the water in a steam-heated domestic hot water tank is controlled by a(n)   11.___

    A. aquastat
    B. thermostatic regulating valve
    C. vacuum breaker
    D. thermostatic trap

12. If scale forms on the seat of a float-operated boiler feedwater regulator, the MOST likely result is   12.___

    A. internal corrosion of the boiler shell
    B. insufficient supply of water to the boiler
    C. flooding of the boiler
    D. shutting down of the oil burner by the low water cutout

13. The compound gauge in the oil suction line shows a high vacuum. This is USUALLY an indication of   13.___

    A. a dirty oil s.trainer
    B. low oil level in the fuel oil storage tank
    C. a leak in the fuel oil preheater
    D. an obstruction in the fuel oil preheater

14. Of the following, the information which is LEAST important on a boiler room log sheet is the   14.___

    A. stack temperature readings
    B. CO_2 readings
    C. number of boilers in operation
    D. boiler room humidity

15. Pitting and corrosion of the water side of the boiler heating surfaces is due MAINLY to the boiler water containing dissolved ⟨15.____⟩

    A. oxygen   B. hydrogen
    C. soda-ash   D. sodium sulphite

16. The combustion efficiency of a boiler can be determined with a CO_2 ⟨16.____⟩

    A. flue gas temperature   B. boiler room humidity
    C. outside air temperature   D. under fire draft

17. The try-cocks of steam boilers are used to ⟨17.____⟩

    A. find the height of water in the boiler
    B. test steam pressure in the boiler
    C. empty the boiler of water
    D. act as safety valves

18. When a spot has burned through the fire bed, it is a GOOD plan to ⟨18.____⟩

    A. fill the burned out hole with green coal
    B. push burning coals to that part of the grate before spreading green coal on it
    C. fill that part of the grate with cold ashes, then place green coal on it
    D. fill the spot with excelsior and then place green coal on it

19. Thin spots or holes in a fire bed are USUALLY ⟨19.____⟩

    A. developed in the front part or center of the fire bed
    B. developed near the back or corners of the fire bed
    C. located where there is a smoky, dull flame
    D. the result of burning soft coal

20. With respect to the operation of univents, the custodian should ⟨20.____⟩

    A. close the steam valve supplying the unit radiators at the close of school every day
    B. see that the steam valve supplying the unit radiators is never closed except when repairs are required
    C. shut off the univents at the close of the day by pulling the main switch
    D. make certain that no part of the univent has water in it

21. Ventilating systems for toilets usually should be separate from the building ventilating system because ⟨21.____⟩

    A. it prevents toilet odors from reaching rooms
    B. toilets need a more dependable ventilating system
    C. the requirements of the two systems are different
    D. only the toilets need ventilating in summer

22. When the flues of a boiler require frequent cleaning, the PROBABLE cause is ⟨22.____⟩

    A. excess draft
    B. too high a rate of combustion
    C. incomplete combustion
    D. lack of clinker formation

23. Generally, the part of a school building where the HIGHEST temperature is maintained in the wintertime is the   23.___

    A. corridors   B. toilets
    C. gymnasium   D. regular classrooms

24. A wet return line is   24.___

    A. one containing air and water
    B. above boiler water level
    C. below boiler water level
    D. a condenser coil

25. A dry return line is   25.___

    A. one containing air *only*
    B. above boiler water level
    C. one containing air and water
    D. a line with a bleeder valve

KEY (CORRECT ANSWERS)

1.	A		11.	B
2.	D		12.	C
3.	D		13.	A
4.	B		14.	D
5.	C		15.	A
6.	D		16.	A
7.	D		17.	A
8.	C		18.	B
9.	A		19.	B
10.	B		20.	B

21.	C
22.	C
23.	D
24.	C
25.	B

TEST 4

DIRECTIONS: Each question or incomplete statement is followed by several suggested answers or completions. Select the one that BEST answers the question or completes the statement. *PRINT THE LETTER OF THE CORRECT ANSWER IN THE SPACE AT THE RIGHT.*

1. The ideal flue gas temperature in a rotary cup oil-fired boiler should be equal to the steam temperature PLUS

    A. 50° F   B. 125° F   C. 275° F   D. 550° F

    1._____

2. The carbon dioxide reading in a boiler flue when the boiler is operating efficiently should be MOST NEARLY

    A. 0.5 inches of water   B. 8 ounces per mol
    C. 10 psi   D. 12 percent

    2._____

3. The one of the following that PRIMARILY indicates a low water level in a steam boiler is the

    A. pressure gauge   B. gauge glass
    C. safety valve   D. hydrometer

    3._____

4. The one of the following steps that should be taken FIRST if a safety valve on a coal-fired steam boiler pops off is to

    A. add water to the boiler
    B. reduce the draft
    C. tap the side of the safety valve with a mallet
    D. open the bottom blow-off valve

    4._____

5. When a custodian finds that the water level of his boiler is dangerously low, he should

    A. open his drafts
    B. immediately fill boiler with cold water
    C. cover the fire with wet ashes
    D. close all air openings to the fire box

    5._____

6. Which one of the following is NOT a good method in banking fires?

    A. A little ash should be left on that portion of the fire not banked.
    B. The coal should be covered with ashes to preserve the fire.
    C. The dampers should be closed except for a small opening to admit a little air.
    D. Ashes should be removed from the ashpit.

    6._____

7. Radiators radiate more heat when they are painted with

    A. bronze paint   B. aluminum paint
    C. regular wall paint   D. shellac

    7._____

8. When a boiler is laid up for the summer, one of the things NOT to do is

    A. tap brace and stary rods with a hammer to detect looserods
    B. leave water in boiler if basement is damp

    8._____

C. close all hand holes and manholes to prevent dust and air from getting into the cleaned boiler

D. clean gauge glasses with muriatic acid to dissolve the accumulations of lime and other deposits

9. The safety device on a gas line is called   9.___

    A. gas cock   B. automatic pilot
    C. solenoid valve   D. safety shut-off valve

10. The MOST efficient boiler fuel operation is   10.___

    A. low CO_2 high CO, low stack gas temperature

    B. high CO_2 low CO, low stack gas temperature

    C. high firebox temperature, high CO_2 high stack temperature

    D. high CO_2 low CO, high stack gas temperature

11. The FIRST thing that should be checked before an oil-fired, low pressure steam boiler is started up in the morning is the   11.___

    A. boiler water level   B. stack temperature
    C. aquastat   D. vaporstat

12. Which of the following types of grates should be used for ease in cleaning fires when hand firing large boilers under natural draft at heavy loads with #1 buckwheat?   12.___

    A. Dumping grates

    B. Stationary grates with 3/4" air spaces

    C. Stationary grates (pinhole type)

    D. Shaking grates

13. A house pump is used to   13.___

    A. drain basements that become flooded

    B. pump sewage from the basement to the sewer

    C. pump city water to a roof storage tank

    D. circulate domestic hot water

14. The device which shuts down an automatic rotary cup oil burner when the steam pressure reaches a preset high limit is a   14.___

    A. pressure gauge   B. pressuretrol
    C. safety valve   D. low water cut-off

15. A pressure gauge connected to a compressed air tank USUALLY reads in   15.___

    A. pounds   B. pounds per square inch
    C. inches of mercury   D. feet of water

16. A badly sooted HRT boiler under coal firing will show a _____ than a clean boiler.   16.___

    A. higher CO_2 value

    B. lower CO_2 value

    C. higher stack temperature

    D. lower draft loss

17. The direct room radiator in a school with a pneumatically controlled steam treating system is cold, while the adjoining rooms are heated adequately.
Of the following, the FIRST thing you would check in the room is the

    A. steam pipe in the room before the pneumatic steam valve
    B. thermostat
    C. pneumatic steam valve
    D. thermostatic trap

17.____

18. In the Ringelmann chart of smoke density, number 4 indicates

    A. the darkest smoke condition
    B. the lightest smoke condition
    C. smoke density of 80 percent
    D. no smoke condition

18.____

19. Of the following, the extinguishing agent that should be used on fires in flammable liquids is

    A. steam   B. water
    C. foam   D. soda and acid

19.____

20. A soda-acid fire extinguisher is recommended for use on fires consisting of

    A. wood or paper
    B. fuel oil or gasoline
    C. electrical causes or fuel oil
    D. paint or turpentine

20.____

Questions 21-23.

DIRECTIONS: Questions 21 through 23 are to be answered on the basis of the following paragraph.

A steam heating system with steam having a pressure of less than 10 pounds is called a low-pressure system. The majority of steam heating systems are of this type. The steam may be provided by low-pressure boilers installed expressly for the purpose, or it may be generated in boilers at a higher pressure and reduced in pressure before admitted to the heating mains. In other instances, it may be possible to use exhaust steam which has been made to run engines and other machines and which still contains enough heat to be utilized in the heating system. The first case represents the system of heating used in the ordinary residence or other small building; the other two represent the systems of heating employed in industrial buildings where a power plant is installed for general power purposes.

21. According to the above paragraph, whether or not a steam heating system is considered a low pressure system is determined by the pressure

    A. generated by the boiler
    B. in the heating main
    C. at the inlet side of the reducing valve
    D. of the exhaust

21.____

22. According to the above paragraph, steam used for Heating is sometimes obtained from steam   22.___

    A.   generated principally to operate machinery
    B.   exhausted from larger boilers
    C.   generated at low pressure and brought up to high pressure before being used
    D.   generated by engines other than boilers

23. As used in the above paragraph, the word *expressly* means   23.___

    A.   rapidly   B.   specifically
    C.   usually   D.   mainly

24. Of the following words, the one that is CORRECTLY spelled is   24.___

    A.   suficient   B.   sufficiant
    C.   sufficient   D.   suficiant

25. Of the following words, the one that is CORRECTLY spelled is   25.___

    A.   fairly   B.   fairley   C.   farely   D.   fairlie

KEY (CORRECT ANSWERS)

1.	B		11.	A
2.	D		12.	A
3.	B		13.	C
4.	B		14.	B
5.	C		15.	B
6.	B		16.	C
7.	B		17.	B
8.	C		18.	C
9.	C		19.	C
10.	B		20.	A

21.	B
22.	A
23.	B
24.	C
25.	A

READING COMPREHENSION
UNDERSTANDING AND INTERPRETING WRITTEN MATERIAL
EXAMINATION SECTION
TEST 1

DIRECTIONS: Each question or incomplete statement is followed by several suggested answers or completions. Select the one that BEST answers the question or completes the statement. *PRINT THE LETTER OF THE CORRECT ANSWER IN THE SPACE AT THE RIGHT.*

Questions 1-2.

DIRECTIONS: Questions 1 and 2 are to be answered SOLELY on the basis of the following paragraph.

When fixing an upper sash cord, you must also remove the lower sash. To do this, the parting strip between the sash must be removed. Now remove the cover from the weight box channel, cut off the cord as before, and pull it over the pulleys. Pull your new cord over the pulleys and down into the channel where it may be fastened to the weight. The cord for an upper sash is cut off 1" or 2" below the pulley with the weight resting on the floor of the pocket and the cord held taut. These measurements allow for slight stretching of the cord. When the cord is cut to length, it can be pulled up over the pulley and tied with a single common knot in the end to fit into the socket in the sash groove. If the knot protrudes beyond the face of the sash, tap it gently to flatten. In this way, it will not become frayed from constant rubbing against the groove.

1. When repairing the upper sash cord, the FIRST thing to do is to   1._____
    A. remove the lower sash
    B. cut the existing sash cord
    C. remove the parting strip
    D. measure the length of new cord necessary

2. According to the above paragraph, the rope may become frayed if the   2._____
    A. pulley is too small   B. knot sticks out
    C. cord is too long   D. weight is too heavy

Questions 3-4.

DIRECTIONS: Questions 3 and 4 are to be answered SOLELY on the basis of the following paragraph.

Repeated burning of the same area should be avoided. Burning should not be done on impervious, shallow, unstable, or highly erodible soils, or on steep slopes—especially in areas subject to heavy rains or rapid snowmelt. When existing vegetation is likely to be killed or seriously weakened by the fire, measures should be taken to assure prompt revegetation of the burned area. Burns should be limited to relatively small proportions of a watershed unit so that the stream channels will be able to carry any increased flows with a minimum of damage.

3. According to the above paragraph, planned burning should be limited to small areas of the watershed because   3._____
   - A. the fire can be better controlled
   - B. existing vegetation will be less likely to be killed
   - C. plants will grow quicker in small areas
   - D. there will be less likelihood of damaging floods

4. According to the above paragraph, burning USUALLY should be done on soils that   4._____
   - A. readily absorb moisture
   - B. have been burnt before
   - C. exist as a thin layer over rock
   - D. can be flooded by nearby streams

Questions 5-11.

DIRECTIONS: Questions 5 through 11 are to be answered SOLELY on the basis of the following paragraph.

FUSE INFORMATION

Badly bent or distorted fuse clips cannot be permitted. Sometimes, the distortion or bending is so slight that it escapes notice, yet it may be the cause for fuse failures through the heat that is developed by the poor contact. Occasionally, the proper spring tension of the fuse clips has been destroyed by overheating from loose wire connections to the clips. Proper contact surfaces must be maintained to avoid faulty operation of the fuse. Maintenance men should remove oxides that form on the copper and brass contacts, check the clip pressure, and make sure that contact surfaces are not deformed or bent in any way. When removing oxides, use a well-worn file and remove only the oxide film. Do not use sandpaper or emery cloth as hard particles may come off and become embedded in the contact surfaces. All wire connections to the fuse holders should be carefully inspected to see that they are tight.

5. Fuse failure because of poor clip contact or loose connections is due to the resulting   5._____
   - A. excessive voltage
   - B. increased current
   - C. lowered resistance
   - D. heating effect

6. Oxides should be removed from fuse contacts by using   6._____
   - A. a dull file
   - B. emery cloth
   - C. fine sandpaper
   - D. a sharp file

7. One result of loose wire connections at the terminal of a fuse clip is stated in the above paragraph to be   7._____
   - A. loss of tension in the wire
   - B. welding of the fuse to the clip
   - C. distortion of the clip
   - D. loss of tension of the clip

8. Simple reasoning will show that the oxide film referred to is undesirable CHIEFLY because it

    A. looks dull
    B. makes removal of the fuse difficult
    C. weakens the clips
    D. introduces undesirable resistance

8._____

9. Fuse clips that are bent very slightly

    A. should be replaced with new clips
    B. should be carefully filed
    C. may result in blowing of the fuse
    D. may prevent the fuse from blowing

9._____

10. From the fuse information paragraph, it would be reasonable to conclude that fuse clips

    A. are difficult to maintain
    B. must be given proper maintenance
    C. require more attention than other electrical equipment
    D. are unreliable

10._____

11. A safe practical way of checking the tightness of the wire connection to the fuse clips of a live 120-volt lighting circuit is to

    A. feel the connection with your hand to see if it is warm
    B. try tightening with an insulated screwdriver or socket wrench
    C. see if the circuit works
    D. measure the resistance with an ohmmeter

11._____

Questions 12-13.

DIRECTIONS: Questions 12 through 13 are to be answered SOLELY on the basis of the following paragraph.

For cast iron pipe lines, the middle ring or sleeve shall have *beveled* ends and shall be high quality cast iron. The middle ring shall have a minimum wall thickness of 3/8" for pipe up to 8", 7/16" for pipe 10" to 30", and 1/2" for pipe over 30", nominal diameter. Minimum length of middle ring shall be 5" for pipe up to 10", 6" for pipe 10" to 30", and 10" for pipe 30" nominal diameter and larger. The middle ring shall not have a center pipe stop, unless otherwise specified.

12. As used in the above paragraph, the word *beveled* means MOST NEARLY

    A. straight   B. slanted   C. curved   D. rounded

12._____

13. In accordance with the above paragraph, the middle ring of a 24" nominal diameter pipe would have a minimum wall thickness and length of _____ thick and _____ long.

    A. 3/8"; 5:   B. 3/8"; 6"
    C. 7/16"; 6"   D. 1/2"; 6"

13._____

Questions 14-17.

DIRECTIONS: Questions 14 through 17 are to be answered SOLELY on the basis of the following paragraph.

Operators spotting loads with long booms and working around men need the smooth, easy operation and positive control of uniform pressure swing clutches. There are no jerks or grabs with these large disc-type clutches because there is always even pressure over the entire clutch lining surface. In the conventional band-type swing clutch, the pressure varies between dead and live ends of the band. The uniform pressure swing clutch has excellent provision for heat dissipation. The driving elements, which are always rotating, have a great number of fins cast in them. This gives them an impeller or blower action for cooling, resulting in longer life and freedom from frequent adjustment.

14. According to the above paragraph, it may be said that conventional band-type swing clutches have   14.____
    A. even pressure on the clutch lining
    B. larger contact area
    C. smaller contact area
    D. uneven pressure on the clutch lining

15. According to the above paragraph, machines equipped with uniform pressure swing clutches will   15.____
    A. give better service under all conditions
    B. require no clutch adjustment
    C. give positive control of hoist
    D. provide better control of swing

16. According to the above paragraph, it may be said that the rotation of the driving elements of the uniform pressure swing clutch is ALWAYS   16.____
    A. continuous   B. constant
    C. varying   D. uncertain

17. According to the above paragraph, freedom from frequent adjustment is due to the   17.____
    A. operator's smooth, easy operation
    B. positive control of the clutch
    C. cooling effect of the rotating fins
    D. larger contact area of the bigger clutch

Questions 18-22.

DIRECTIONS: Questions 18 through 22 are to be answered SOLELY on the basis of the following paragraphs.

Exhaust valve clearance adjustment on diesel engines is very important for proper operation of the engine. Insufficient clearance between the exhaust valve stem and the rocker arm causes a loss of compression and, after a while, burning of the valves and valve seat inserts. On the other hand, too much valve clearance will result in noisy operation of the engine.

Exhaust valves that are maintained in good operating condition will result in efficient combustion in the engine. Valve seats must be true and unpitted, and valve stems must work smoothly within the valve guides. Long valve life will result from proper maintenance and operation of the engine.

Engine operating temperatures should be maintained between 160°F and 185°F. Low operating temperatures result in incompl ete combustion and the deposit of fuel lacquers on valves.

18. According to the above paragraphs, too much valve clearance will cause the engine to operate

    A. slowly   B. noisily   C. smoothly   D. cold

18._____

19. On the basis of the information given in the above paragraphs, operating temperatures of a diesel engine should be between

    A. 125°F and 130°F   B. 140°F and 150°F
    C. 160°F and 185°F   D. 190°F and 205°F

19._____

20. According to the above paragraphs, the deposit of fuel lacquers on valves is caused by

    A. high operating temperatures
    B. insufficient valve clearance
    C. low operating temperatures
    D. efficient combustion

20._____

21. According to the above paragraphs, for efficient operation of the engine, valve seats must

    A. have sufficient clearance
    B. be true and unpitted
    C. operate at low temperatures
    D. be adjusted regularly

21._____

22. According to the above paragraphs, a loss of compression is due to insufficient clearance between the exhaust valve stem and the

    A. rocker arm   B. valve seat
    C. valve seat inserts   D. valve guides

22._____

Questions 23-25.

DIRECTIONS: Questions 23 through 25 are to be answered SOLELY on the basis of the following excerpt:

A SPECIFICATION FOR ELECTRIC WORK FOR THE CITY

Breakers shall be equipped with magnetic blowout coils...Handles of breakers shall be trip-free...Breakers shall be designed to carry 100% of trip rating continuously; to have inverse time delay tripping above 100% of trip rating...

23. According to the above paragraph, the breaker shall have provision for

    A. resetting   B. arc quenching
    C. adjusting trip time   D. adjusting trip rating

23._____

24. According to the above paragraph, the breaker

    A. shall trip easily at exactly 100% of trip rating
    B. shall trip instantly at a little more than 100% of trip rating
    C. should be constructed so that it shall not be possible to prevent it from opening on overload or short circuit by holding the handle in the ON position
    D. shall not trip prematurely at 100% of trip rating

24._____

25. According to the above paragraph, the breaker shall trip
    A. instantaneously as soon as 100% of trip rating is reached
    B. instantaneously as soon as 100% of trip rating is exceeded
    C. more quickly the greater the current, once 100% of trip rating is exceeded
    D. after a predetermined fixed time lapse, once 100% of trip rating is reached

25._____

——————

KEY (CORRECT ANSWERS)

1.	C		11.	B
2.	B		12.	B
3.	D		13.	C
4.	A		14.	D
5.	D		15.	D
6.	A		16.	A
7.	D		17.	C
8.	D		18.	B
9.	C		19.	C
10.	B		20.	C

21.	B
22.	A
23.	B
24.	C
25.	C

——————

TEST 2

DIRECTIONS: Each question or incomplete statement is followed by several suggested answers or completions. Select the one that BEST answers the question or completes the statement. *PRINT THE LETTER OF THE CORRECT ANSWER IN THE SPACE AT THE RIGHT.*

Questions 1-4.

DIRECTIONS: Questions 1 through 4 are to be answered SOLELY on the basis of the following paragraph.

A low pressure hot water boiler shall include a relief valve or valves of a capacity such that with the heat generating equipment operating at maximum, the pressure cannot rise more than 20 percent above the maximum allowable working pressure (set pressure) if that is 30 p.s.i. gage or less, nor more than 10 percent if it is more than 30 p.s.i. gage. The difference between the set pressure and the pressure at which the valve is relieving is known as *over-pressure or accumulation.* If the steam relieving capacity in pounds per hour is calculated, it shall be determined by dividing by 1,000 the maximum BTU output at the boiler nozzle obtainable from the heat generating equipment, or by multiplying the square feet of heating surface by five.

1. In accordance with the above paragraph, the capacity of a relief valve should be computed on the basis of   1._____
   - A. size of boiler
   - B. maximum rated capacity of generating equipment
   - C. average output of the generating equipment
   - D. minimum capacity of generating equipment

2. In accordance with the above paragraph, with a set pressure of 30 p.s.i. gage, the overpressure should not be more than _____ p.s.i.   2._____
   - A. 3   B. 6   C. 33   D. 36

3. In accordance with the above paragraph, a relief valve should start relieving at a pressure equal to the   3._____
   - A. set pressure
   - B. over pressure
   - C. over pressure minus set pressure
   - D. set pressure plus over pressure

4. In accordance with the above paragraph, the steam relieving capacity can be computed by   4._____
   - A. *multiplying* the maximum BTU output by 5
   - B. *dividing* the pounds of steam per hour by 1,000
   - C. *dividing* the maximum BTU output by the square feet of heating surface
   - D. *dividing* the maximum BTU output by 1,000

Questions 5-8.

DIRECTIONS: Questions 5 through 8 are to be answered SOLELY on the basis of the following paragraph.

Air conditioning units requiring a minimum rate of flow of water in excess of one-half (1/2) gallon per minute shall be metered. Air conditioning equipment with a refrigeration unit which has a definite rate of capacity in tons or fractions thereof, the charge will be at the rate of $30 per annum per ton capacity from the date installed to the date when the supply is metered. Such units, when equipped with an approved water-conserving device, shall be charged at the rate of $4.50 per annum per ton capacity from the date installed to the date when the supply is metered.

5.   A man who was in the market for air conditioning equipment was considering three different units. Unit 1 required a flow of 28 gallons of water per hour; Unit 2 required 30 gallons of water per hour; Unit 3 required 32 gallons of water per hour. The man asked the salesman which units would require the installation of a water meter. According to the above passage, the salesman SHOULD answer:
      A.   All three units require meters
      B.   Units 2 and 3 require meters
      C.   Unit 3 only requires a meter
      D.   None of the units require a meter

5._____

6.   Suppose that air conditioning equipment with a refrigeration unit of 10 tons was put in operation on October 1; and in the following year on July 1, a meter was installed. According to the above passage, the charge for this period would be _____ the annual rate.
      A.   twice   B.   equal to
      C.   three-fourths   D.   one-fourth

6._____

7.   The charge for air conditioning equipment which has no refrigeration unit
      A.   is $30 per year
      B.   is $25.50 per year
      C.   is $4.50 per year
      D.   cannot be determined from the above passage

7._____

8.   The charge for air conditioning equipment with a seven-ton refrigeration unit equipped with an approved water-conserving device
      A.   is $4.50 per year
      B.   is $25.50 per year
      C.   is $31.50 per year
      D.   cannot be determined from the above passage

8._____

Questions 9-14.

DIRECTIONS: Questions 9 through 14 are to be answered SOLELY on the basis of the following paragraph.

The city makes unremitting efforts to keep the water free from pollution. An inspectional force under a sanitary expert is engaged in patrolling the watersheds to see that the department's sanitary regulations are observed. Samples taken daily from various points in the water supply system are examined and analyzed at the three laboratories maintained by the department. All water before delivery to the distribution mains is treated with chlorine to destroy bacteria. In addition, some water is aerated to free it from gases and, in some cases, from microscopic organisms. Generally, microscopic organisms which develop in the reservoirs and at times impart an unpleasant taste and odor to the water, though in no sense harmful to health, are destroyed by treatment with copper sulfate and by chlorine dosage. None of the supplies is filtered, but the quality of the water supplied by the city is excellent for all purposes, and it is clear and wholesome.

9. According to the above paragraph, microscopic organisms are removed from the water supplied to the city by means of 　　　　　　　9._____
    A.   chlorine alone
    B.   chlorine, aeration, and filtration
    C.   chlorine, aeration, filtration, and sampling
    D.   copper sulfate, chlorine, and aeration

10. Microscopic organisms in the water supply GENERALLY are 　　　　　10._____
    A.   a health menace   B.   impossible to detect
    C.   not harmful to health   D.   not destroyed in the water

11. The MAIN function of the inspectional force, as described in the above paragraph, is to 　　　　　　　11._____
    A.   take samples of water for analysis
    B.   enforce sanitary regulations
    C.   add chlorine to the water supply
    D.   inspect water-use meters

12. According to the above paragraph, chlorine is added to water before entering the 　　　　　　　12._____
    A.   watersheds   B.   reservoirs
    C.   distribution mains   D.   run-off areas

13. Of the following suggested headings or titles for the above paragraph, the one that BEST tells what the paragraph is about is 　　　　　13._____
    A.   QUALITY OF WATER   B.   CHLORINATION OF WATER
    C.   TESTING OF WATER   D.   BACTERIA IN WATER

14. The MOST likely reason for taking samples of water for examination and analysis from various points in the water supply system is: 　　　　14._____
    A.   The testing points are convenient to the department's laboratories
    B.   Water from one part of the system may be made undrinkable by a local condition
    C.   The samples can be distributed equally among the three laboratories
    D.   The hardness or softness of water varies from place to place

Questions 15-17.

DIRECTIONS: Questions 15 through 17 are to be answered SOLELY on the basis of the following paragraph.

A building measuring 200' x 100' at the street is set back 20' on all sides at the 15th floor, and an additional 10' on all sides at the 30th floor. The building is 35 stories high.

15. The floor area of the 16th floor is MOST NEARLY _____ sq. ft.   15.____
    A. 20,000   B. 14,400   C. 9,600   D. 7,500

16. The floor area of the 35th floor is MOST NEARLY _____ sq. ft.   16.____
    A. 20,000   B. 13,900   C. 7,500   D. 5,600

17. The floor area of the 16th floor, compared to the floor area of the 2nd floor, is   17.____
MOST NEARLY _____ as much.
    A. three-fourths (3/4)   B. two-thirds (2/3)
    C. one-half (1/2)   D. four-tenths (4/10)

Question 18.

DIRECTIONS: Question 18 is to be answered SOLELY on the basis of the following
paragraph.

Experience has shown that, in general, a result of the installation of meters on services not previously metered is to reduce the amount of water consumed, but is not necessarily to reduce the peak load on plumbing systems. The permissible head loss through meters at their rated maximum flow is 20 p.s.i. The installation of a meter may therefore appreciably lower the pressures available in fixtures on a plumbing system.

18. According to the above paragraph, a water meter may   18.____
    A. limit the flow in the plumbing system of 20 p.s.i.
    B. reduce the peak load on the plumbing system
    C. increase the overall amount of water consumed
    D. reduce the pressure in the plumbing system

Question 19.

DIRECTIONS: Question 19 is to be answered SOLELY on the basis of the following
paragraph.

Spring comes without trumpets to a city. The asphalt is a wilderness that does not quicken overnight; winds blow gritty with cinders instead of merry with the smells of earth and fertilizer. Women wear their gardens on their hats. But spring is a season in the city, and it has its own harbingers, constant as daffodils. Shop windows change their colors, people walk more slowly on the streets, what one can see of the sky has a bluer tone. Pulitzer prizes awake and sing and matinee tickets go-a-begging. But gayer than any of these are the carousels, which are already in sheltered places, beginning to turn with the sound of springtime itself. They are the earliest and the truest and the oldest of all the urban signs.

19. In the passage above, the word *harbingers* means   19.____
    A. storms   B. truths   C. virtues   D. forerunners

Questions 20-22.

DIRECTIONS: Questions 20 through 22 are to be answered SOLELY on the basis
of the following paragraph.

Gas heaters include manually operated, automatic, and instantaneous heaters. Some heaters are equipped with a thermostat which controls the fuel supply so that when the water falls below a predetermined temperature, the fuel is automatically turned on. In some types, the hot-water storage tank is well-insulated to economize the use of fuel. Instantaneous heaters are arranged so that the opening of a faucet on the hot-water pipe will increase the flow of fuel, which is ignited by a continuously burning pilot light to heat the water to from 120° to 130°F. The possibility that the pilot light will die out offers a source of danger in the use of automatic appliances which depend on a pilot light. Gas and oil heaters are dangerous, and they should be designed to prevent the accumulation, in a confined space within the heater, of a large volume of an explosive mixture.

20. According to the above passage, the opening of a hot-water faucet on a hot-water pipe connected to an instantaneous hot-water heater will the pilot light.   20._____
    A.   *increase* the temperature of
    B.   *increase* the flow of fuel to
    C.   *decrease* the flow of fuel to
    D.   *have a marked effect* on

21. According to the above passage, the fuel is automatically turned on in a heater equipped with a thermostat whenever   21._____
    A.   the water temperature drops below 120°F
    B.   the pilot light is lit
    C.   the water temperature drops below some predetermined temperature
    D.   a hot water supply is opened

22. According to the above passage, some hot-water storage tanks are well-insulated to   22._____
    A.   accelerate the burning of the fuel
    B.   maintain the water temperature between 120° and 130°F
    C.   prevent the pilot light from being extinguished
    D.   minimize the expenditure of fuel

Question 23.

DIRECTIONS: Question 23 is to be answered SOLELY on the basis of the following paragraph.

Breakage of the piston under high-speed operation has been the commonest fault of disc piston meters. Various techniques are adopted to prevent this, such as *throttling* the meter, cutting away the edge of the piston, or reinforcing it, but these are simply makeshifts.

23. As used in the above paragraph, the word *throttling* means MOST NEARLY   23._____
    A.   enlarging   B.   choking
    C.   harnessing   D.   dismantling

Questions 24-25.

DIRECTIONS: Questions 24 and 25 are to be answered SOLELY on the basis of the following paragraph.

One of the most common and objectionable difficulties occurring in a drainage system is trap seal loss. This failure can be attributed directly to inadequate ventilation of the trap and the subsequent negative and positive pressures which occur. A trap seal may be lost either by siphonage and/or back pressure. Loss of the trap seal by siphonage is the result of a negative pressure in the drainage system. The seal content of the trap is forced by siphonage into the waste piping of the drainage system through exertion of atmospheric pressure on the fixture side of the trap seal.

24. According to the above paragraph, a positive pressure is a direct result of   24._____
     A.   siphonage   B.   unbalanced trap seal
     C.   poor ventilation   D.   atmospheric pressure

25. According to the above paragraph, the water in the trap is forced into the drain   25._____
pipe by
     A.   atmospheric pressure   B.   back pressure
     C.   negative pressure   D.   back pressure on fixture side of seal

KEY (CORRECT ANSWERS)

1.	B		11.	B
2.	B		12.	C
3.	D		13.	A
4.	D		14.	B
5.	C		15.	C
6.	C		16.	D
7.	D		17.	C
8.	C		18.	D
9.	D		19.	B
10.	C		20.	B

21.	C
22.	D
23.	B
24.	C
25.	A

HEATING AND ENVIRONMENTAL CONTROL

CONTENTS

HEATING AND ENVIRONMENTAL CONTROL

I. Introduction

The function of a heating system is to provide for human comfort. The variables to be controlled are temperature, air motion, and relative humidity. Temperature must be maintained uniformly throughout the heated area. Field experience indicates a variation from 6 to 10 degrees F from floor to ceiling. The adequacy of the heating device and the tightness of the structure or room determine the degree of personal comfort within the dwelling.

Coal, wood, oil, gas, and electricity are the main sources of heat energy. Heating systems commonly used are steam, hot water, and hot air. The housing inspector should have a knowledge of the various heating fuels and systems to be able to determine their adequacy and safety in operation. To cover fully all aspects of the heating system, the entire area and physical components of the system must be considered.

II. Definitions

A **Anti-flooding Control** — A safety control that shuts off fuel and ignition when excessive fuel accumulates in the appliance.

B **Appliance:**
 1 **High-heat** — a unit that operates with flue entrance temperature of combustion products above 1,500°F.

 2 **Medium heat** — same as high-heat, except above 600°F.

 3 **Low heat** — same as high heat, except below 600°F.

C **Boiler:**
 1 **High pressure** – a boiler furnishing pressure at 15 psi or more.
 2 **Low pressure** — (hot water or steam) — a boiler furnishing steam at a pressure less than 15 psi or hot water not more than 30 psi.

D **Burner** — A device that provides the mixing of fuel, air, and ignition in a combustion chamber.

E **Chimney** — A vertical shaft containing one or more passageways.
 1 **Factory-built chimney** — a tested and accredited flue for venting gas appliances, incinerators and solid or liquid fuel-burning appliances.

 2 **Masonry chimney** — a field-constructed chimney built of masonry and lined with terra cotta flue or firebrick.

 3 **Metal chimney** — a field-constructed chimney of metal.

 4 **Chimney Connector** — A pipe or breeching that connects the heating appliance to the chimney.

F **Clearance** — The distance separating the appliance, chimney connector, plenum, and flue from the nearest surface of combustible material.

G **Central Heating System** — A boiler or furnace, flue connected, installed as an integral part of the structure and designed to supply heat adequately for the structure.

H **Controls:**
 1 **High-low limit control** — an automatic control that responds to liquid level changes and pressure or temperature changes and that limits operation of the appliance to be controlled.

2 Primary safety control — the automatic safety control intended to prevent abnormal discharge of fuel at the burner in case of ignition failure or flame failure.

3 Combustion safety control — a primary safety control that responds to flame properties, sensing the presence of flame and causing fuel to be shut off in event of flame failure.

I Convector — A convector is a radiator that supplies a maximum amount of heat by convection, using many closely-spaced metal fins fitted onto pipes that carry hot water or steam and thereby heat the circulating air.

J Conversion — a boiler or furnace, flue connected, originally designed for solid fuel but converted for liquid or gas fuel.

K Damper — a valve for regulating draft. Generally located on the exhaust side of the combustion chamber, usually in the chimney connector.

L Draft Hood — a device placed in and made a part of the vent connector (chimney connector or smoke pipe) from an appliance, or in the appliance itself, that is designed to (a) ensure the ready escape of the products of combustion in the event of no draft, back-draft, or stoppage beyond the draft hood; (b) prevent backdraft from entering the appliance; (c) neutralize the effect of stack action of the chimney flue upon appliance operation.

M Draft Regulator — a device that functions to maintain a desired draft in oil-fired appliances by automatically reducing the chimney draft to the desired value. Sometimes this device is referred to, in the field, as air-balance, air-stat, or flue velocity control.

N Fuel Oil — a liquid mixture or compound derived from petroleum that does not emit flammable vapor below a temperature of 125°F.

O Heat — the warming of a building, apartment, or room by a stove, furnace, or electricity.

P Heating Plant — the furnace, boiler, or the other heating devices used to generate steam, hot water, or hot air, which then is circulated through a distribution system. It uses coal, gas, oil, or wood as its source of heat.

Q Limit Control — a thermostatic device installed in the duct system to shut off the supply of heat at a predetermined temperature of the circulated air.

R Oil Burner — a device for burning oil in heating appliances such as boilers, furnaces, water heaters, and ranges. A burner of this type may be a pressure-atomizing gun type, a horizontal or vertical rotary type, or a mechanical or natural draft-vaporizing type.

S Oil Stove — a flue-connected, self-contained, self-supporting oil-burning range or room heater equipped with an integral tank not exceeding 10 gallons; it may be designed to be connected to a separate oil supply tank.

T Plenum Chamber — an air compartment to which one or more distributing air ducts are connected.

U Pump, Automatic Oil — a device that automatically pumps oil from the supply tank and delivers it in specific quantities to an oil-burning appliance. The pump or device is designed to stop pumping automatically in case of a breakage of the oil supply line.

V Radiant Heat — a method of heating a building by means of electric coils, hot water, or steam pipes installed in the floors, walls, or ceilings.

W **Register** — a grille-covered opening in a floor or wall through which hot or cold air can be introduced into a room. It may or may not be arranged to permit closing of the grille.

X **Room Heater** — a self-contained, free-standing heating appliance intended for installation in the space being heated and not intended for duct connection (space heater).

Y **Smoke Detector** — a device installed in the plenum chamber or in the main supply air duct of an air-conditioning system to shut off the blower automatically and close a fire damper in the presence of smoke.

Z **Tank** — a separate tank connected, directly or by pump, to an oil-burning appliance.

AA **Thimble** — a term applied to a metal or terra cotta lining for a chimney or furnace pipe.

BB **Valve — Main Shut-off Valve** — a manually operated valve in an oil line for the purpose of turning on or off the oil supply to the burner.

CC **Vent System** — the gas vent or chimney and vent connector, if used, assembled to form a continuous, unobstructed passageway from the gas appliance to the outside atmosphere for the purpose of removing vent gases.

III. Fuels

A Coal

Classification and composition — the four types of coal are: anthracite, bituminous, sub-bituminous, and lignitic.

Coal is prepared in many sizes and combinations of sizes. The combustible portions of the coal are fixed carbons, volatile matter (hydrocarbons), and small amounts of sulfur.

In combination with these are non-combustible elements composed of moisture and impurities that form ash. The various types differ in heat content. The heat content is determined by analysis and is expressed in British Thermal Units (BTU) per pound. The type and size of coal used are determined by the availability and by the equipment in which it is burned.

The type and size of coal must be proper for the particular heating unit; that is, the furnace grate and flue size must be designed for the particular type of coal. Excessive coal gas can be generated through improper firing as a result of improper fuel or improper furnace design, or both.

The owner should be questioned about his procedure for adding coal to his furnace. It should be explained that a period of time must be allowed to pass before damping to prevent the release of excessive coal gas. This should also be done before damping for the night or other periods when full draft is not required.

Improper coal furnace operation can result in an extremely hazardous and unhealthful occupancy — the inspector should be able to offer helpful operational procedures. Ventilation of the area surrounding the furnace is very important in order to prevent heat buildup and to supply air for combustion.

B Fuel Oil

Fuel oils are derived from petroleum, which consists primarily of compounds of hydrogen and carbon (hydrocarbons) and smaller amounts of nitrogen and sulfur.

Classification of fuel oils Domestic fuel oils are controlled by rigid specifications. Six grades of fuel oil are generally used in healing systems; the lighter two grades are used primarily for domestic heating.

These grades are:

1   **Grade Number 1** — A volatile, distillate oil for use in burners that prepare fuel for burning solely by vaporization (oil-fired space heaters).

2   **Grade Number 2** — A moderate-weight, volatile, distillate oil used for burners that prepare oil for burning by a combination of vaporization and atomization. This grade of oil is commonly used in domestic heating furnaces.

3   **Grade Number 3** — A low-viscosity, distillate oil used in burners wherein fuel and air are prepared for burning solely by atomization.

4   **Grade Number 4** — A medium-viscosity oil used in burners without preheating. (Small industrial or apartment house applications.)

5   **Grade Number 5** — A medium-viscosity oil used in burners with preheaters that require an oil of lower viscosity than Grade Number 6. (Industrial or apartment house application.)

6   **Grade Number 6** — A high-viscosity oil for use in burners with preheating facilities adequate for handling oil of high viscosity. (Industrial applications.)

7   **Heat content** — Heating values of oil vary from approximately 152,000 BTU per gallon for Number 6 oil to 136,000 BTU per gallon for Number 1.

Oil is more widely used today than coal and provides a more automatic source of heat and comfort. It also requires more complicated systems and controls.

If the oil supply is used within the basement or cellar area, certain basic regulations must be followed (see Figure 1). No more than two 275-gallon tanks may be installed above ground in the lowest story of any one building. The tank shall not be closer than 7 feet horizontally to any boiler, furnace, stove, or exposed flame. Fuel oil lines should be embedded in a concrete or cement floor or protected against damage if they run across the floor. Bach tank must have a shutoff valve that will stop the flow from each tank if a leak develops in the line to or in the burner itself.

The tank or tanks must be vented to the outside, and a gauge showing the quantity of oil in the tank or tanks must be tight and operative. Tanks must be off the floor and on a stable base to prevent settlement or movement that may rupture the connections.

A buried outside tank installation is shown in Figure 2.

C Gas

Commercial gas fuels are colorless gases. Some have a characteristic pungent odor, while others are odorless and cannot be detected by smell. Although gas fuels are easily handled in heating equipment, their presence in air in appreciable quantities becomes a serious health hazard. Gases diffuse readily in the air, making explosive mixtures possible. (A proportion of combustible gas and air that is ignited burns with such a high velocity that an explosive force is created.) Because of these characteristics of gas fuels, precautions must be taken to prevent leaks, and care must be exercised when gas-fired equipment is lit.

Classification of gas - Gas is broadly classified as natural or manufactured.

1.   **Manufactured Gas** — This gas as distributed is usually a combination of certain proportions of gases produced by two or more processes as obtained from coke, coal, and petroleum. Its BTU value per cubic foot is generally closely regulated, and costs are determined on a guaran-

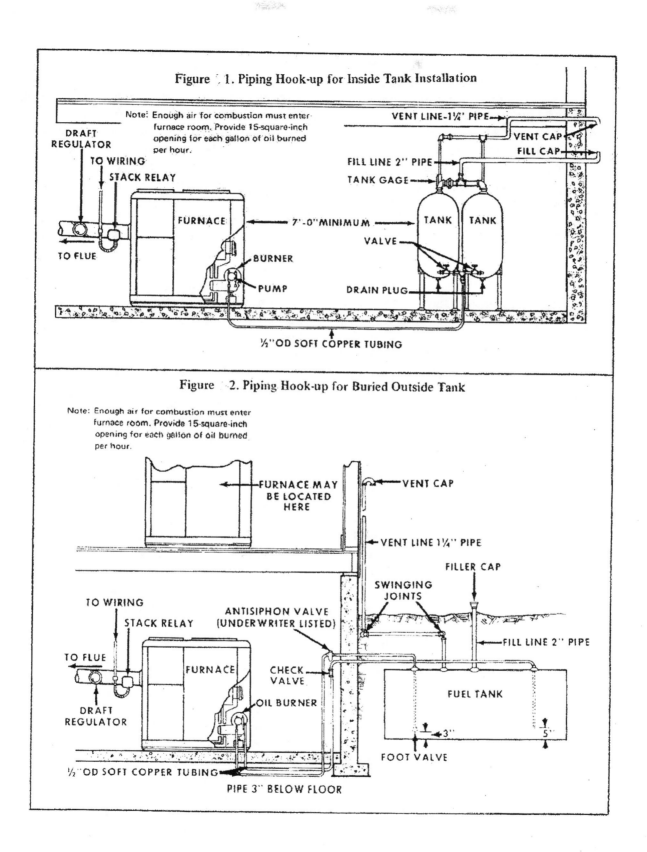

Figure 1. Piping Hook-up for Inside Tank Installation

Note: Enough air for combustion must enter furnace room. Provide 15-square-inch opening for each gallon of oil burned per hour.

DRAFT REGULATOR

TO WIRING

STACK RELAY

TO FLUE

FURNACE

BURNER

PUMP

7'-0" MINIMUM

VENT LINE-1¼' PIPE

VENT CAP

FILL CAP

FILL LINE 2" PIPE

TANK GAGE

TANK   TANK

VALVE

DRAIN PLUG

½"OD SOFT COPPER TUBING

Figure 2. Piping Hook-up for Buried Outside Tank

Note: Enough air for combustion must enter furnace room. Provide 15-square-inch opening for each gallon of oil burned per hour.

FURNACE MAY BE LOCATED HERE

VENT CAP

VENT LINE 1¼" PIPE

FILLER CAP

TO WIRING

STACK RELAY

TO FLUE

DRAFT REGULATOR

FURNACE

ANTISIPHON VALVE (UNDERWRITER LISTED)

OIL BURNER

CHECK VALVE

SWINGING JOINTS

FILL LINE 2" PIPE

FUEL TANK

FOOT VALVE

3"

5"

½"OD SOFT COPPER TUBING

PIPE 3" BELOW FLOOR

teed BTU basis, usually 520 to 540 per cubic foot.

2. **Natural Gas** — This gas is a mixture of several combustible and inert gases. It is one of the richest gases and is obtained from wells ordinarily located in petroleum-producing areas. The heat content may vary from 700 to 1,300 BTU's per cubic foot with a generally accepted average figure of 1,000 BTU's per cubic foot. Natural gases are distributed through pipe lines to point of utilization and are often mixed with manufactured gas to maintain a guaranteed BTU content.

3. **Liquified Petroleum Gas** — Principal products of liquified petroleum gas are butane and propane. Butane and propane are derived from natural gas or petroleum refinery gas and are chemically classified as hydrocarbon gases.

Specifically, butane and propane are on the borderline between a liquid and a gaseous state. At ordinary atmospheric pressure butane is a gas above 33°F and propane a gas at -42°F. These gases are mixed to produce commercial gas suitable for various climatic conditions. Butane and propane are heavier than air. The heat content of butane is 3,274 BTU's per cubic foot while that of propane is 2,519.

The gas burner should be equipped with an automatic cutoff in case the flame fails. Shutoff valves should be located within 1 foot of the burner connection and on the output side of the meter.

CAUTION — Liquified petroleum gas is heavier than air; therefore, the gas will accumulate at the bottom of confined areas. If a leak should develop, care should be taken to ventilate the appliance before lighting.

D Electricity

Electricity is gaining popularity in many regions, particularly where costs are competitive with other sources of heat energy. With an electric system, the housing inspector should rely mainly on the electrical inspector for proper installation. There are a few items, however, to be concerned with to ensure safe use of the equipment. Check to see that the units are accredited testing agency approved and installed according to the manufacturer's specifications. Most convector-type units are required to be installed at least 2 inches above the floor level, not only to ensure that proper convection currents are established through the unit, but also to allow sufficient air insulation from any combustible flooring material. The housing inspector should check for curtains that extend too close to the unit or loose, long pile rugs that are too close. A distance of 6 inches on the floor and 12 inches on the walls should separate rug or curtains from the appliance.

Radiant heating plastered into the ceiling or wall is technical in nature and not a part of the housing inspector's competence. He should, however, be knowledgeable about the system used. These systems are relatively new. If wires are bared in the plastering they should be treated as open and exposed wiring.

IV. Central Heating Units

The boiler should be placed in a separate room whenever possible; in new construction this is usually required. In most housing inspections, however, we are dealing with existing conditions; therefore, we must adapt the situation as closely as possible to acceptable safety standards. In many old buildings the furnace is located in the center of the cellar or basement, and this location does not lend itself for practical conversion to a boiler room.

A Boiler Location

Consider the physical requirements for a boiler room.

1 Ventilation — More circulating air is required for the boiler room than for a habitable room, in order to reduce the heat buildup caused by the boiler or furnace as well as to supply oxygen for combustion.

2 Fire Protection Rating — As specified by various codes (fire code, building code, and insurance underwriters) the fire regulations must be strictly adhered to in areas surrounding the boiler or furnace. This minimum dimension from which a boiler or furnace is to be spaced from a wall or ceiling is shown in Figure 3.

Many times the enclosure of the furnace or boiler creates a problem of providing adequate air supply and ventilation for the room. Where codes and local authority permit, it may be more practical to place the furnace or boiler in an open area. The ceiling above the furnace should be fire protected to a distance of 3 feet beyond all furnace or boiler appurtenances and this area should be free of all storage material. The furnace or boiler should be set on a firm foundation of concrete if located in the cellar or basement. If the codes permit furnace installations on the first floor, then the building code must be consulted for proper setting and location.

B Heating Boilers

Boilers may be classified according to several kinds of characteristics. The material may be cast iron or steel. Their construction may be section, portable, fire-tube, water-tube, or special. Domestic heating boilers are generally of low-pressure type with a maximum working pressure of 15 pounds per square inch for steam and 30 pounds per square inch for hot water.

All boilers have a combustion chamber for burning fuel. Automatic fuel-firing devices help supply the fuel and control the combustion. Handfiring is accomplished by the provision of a grate, ash pit, and controllable drafts to admit air under the fuel bed and over it through slots in the firing door. A check draft is required at the smoke pipe connection to control chimney draft. The gas passes from the combustion chamber to the flue, passages (smoke pipe) designed for maximum possible transfer of heat from the gas. Provisions must be made for cleaning flue passages.

The term boiler is applied to the single heat source that can supply either steam or hot-water (boiler is often called a heater).

Cast iron boilers are generally classified as:
1 Square or rectangular boilers with vertical sections.
2 Round, square, or rectangular boilers with horizontal pancake sections.

Cast iron boilers are usually shipped in sections and assembled at the site.

C Steel Boilers

Most steel boilers are assembled units with welded steel construction and are called portable boilers. Larger boilers are installed in refractory brick settings built on the site. Above the combustion chamber a group of tubes is suspended, usually horizontally, between two headers. If flue gases pass through the tubes and water surrounds them, the boiler is designated as the fire-tube type. When water flows through the tubes, it is termed water-tube. Fire-tube is the predominant type.

D Heating Furnaces

Heating furnaces are the heat sources used when air is the heat-carrying medium. When air circulates because of the different densities of the heated and cooled air, the furnace is a gravity type. A fan may be included for the air circulation; this type is called a mechanical warm-air furnace. Furnaces may be of cast iron or steel and burn various types of fuel.

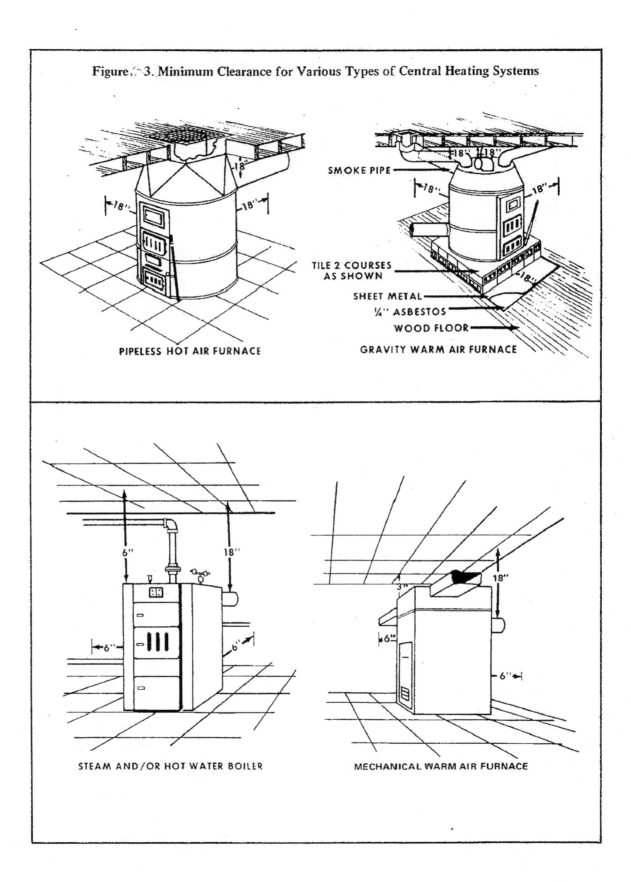

Figure 3. Minimum Clearance for Various Types of Central Heating Systems

PIPELESS HOT AIR FURNACE

GRAVITY WARM AIR FURNACE

SMOKE PIPE
TILE 2 COURSES AS SHOWN
SHEET METAL
¼" ASBESTOS
WOOD FLOOR

STEAM AND/OR HOT WATER BOILER

MECHANICAL WARM AIR FURNACE

V. Fuel-Burning Procedures and Automatic Firing Equipment

A Coal — Many localities throughout the nation still use coal as a heating fuel.

1 Hand Stoking - In many older furnaces, the coal is stoked or fed into the fire box by hand.

2 Automatic Stokers - The single-retort, underfeed-type bituminous coal stoker is the most commonly used domestic-type steam or hot water boiler (see Figure 4). The stoker consists of a coal hopper, a screw for conveying coal from hopper to retort, a fan that supplies air for combustion, a transmission for driving coalfeed and fan, and an electric motor for supplying power. The air for combustion is admitted to the fuel through tuyeres at the top of the retort. The stoker feeds coal to the furnace intermittently in accordance with the temperature or pressure demands.

B Oil Burners — Oil burners are broadly designated as distillate, domestic, and commercial or industrial. Distillate burners are usually found in oil-fired space heaters. Domestic oil burners are usually power driven and are used in domestic heating plants. Commercial or industrial burners are used in larger central-heating plants for steam or power generation.

1 Domestic Oil Burners — Thesevaporize and atomize the oil, and deliver a predetermined quantity of oil and air to the combustion chambers. Domestic oil burners operate automatically to maintain a desired temperature.

a Gun-type burners — These burners atomize the oil either by oil pressure or by low-pressure air forced through a nozzle.

The oil system pressure atomizing burner (see Figure 5) consists of a strainer, pump, pressure-regulating valve, shutoff valve, and atomizing nozzle. The air system consists of a power-drive fan and an air tube that surrounds the nozzle and electrode assembly. The fan and oil pump are generally connected directly to the motor. Oil pressures normally used are about 100 pounds per square inch, but pressures con-

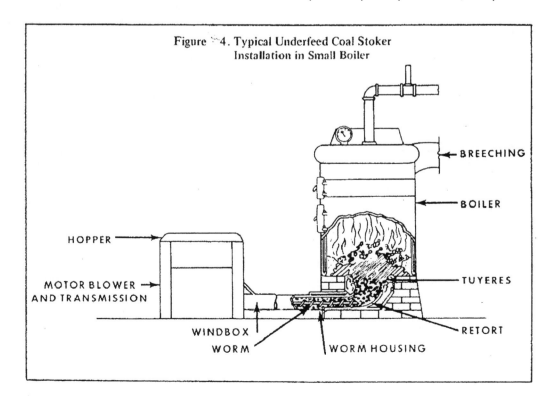

Figure 4. Typical Underfeed Coal Stoker Installation in Small Boiler

siderably in excess of this are sometimes used.

The form and parts of low-pressure air-atomizing burners (see Figure 5), are similar to high-pressure atomizing burners except for addition of a small air pump, and a different way of delivering air and oil to the nozzle or orifice.

b Vertical rotary burners - The atomizing-type burner, sometimes known as a radiant or suspended-flame burner, atomizes oil by throwing it from the circumference of a rapidly rotating motor-driven cup. The burner is installed so that the driving parts are protected from the heat of the flame by a hearth of refractory material at about the grate elevation. Oil is fed by pump or gravity, while the draft is mechanical or a combination of natural and mechanical.

c Horizontal rotary burners These were originally designed for commercial and industrial use but are available in sizes suitable for domestic use. In this burner, oil is atomized by being thrown in a

Figure 5. Cut-Away of Typical
High-Pressure Gun-Burner

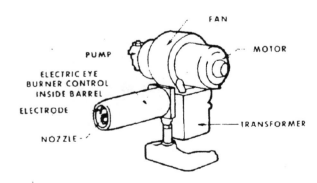

conical spray from a rapidly rotating cup. Horizontal rotary burners employ electric-gas or gas-pilot ignition and operate with a wide range of fuels, primarily with Numbers 1 and 2 fuel oil. Primary safety controls for burner operation are. necessary. An anti-flooding device must be a part of the sys-

tem so that, if ignition in the burner should fail, the oil will not continue to flow. Likewise, a stack control is necessary to shut off the burner if the stack temperatures become excessive. A reset button on the older stack control units releases if excessive (predetermined) temperatures are exceeded and thus cuts off all power to the burner. This button must be reset before starting can be attempted. The newer models now use electric eye-type control on the burner itself.

2 Ignition — On the basis of the method employed to ignite fuels, burners are divided into five groups as follows:

a Electric — A high-voltage electric spark is made in the path of an oil and air mixture and this causes ignition. This electric spark may be continuous or may be in operation only long enough to ignite the oil. Electric ignition is almost universally used. Electrodes are located near the nozzles (see Figure 5) but not in the path of the oil spray.

b Gas pilot — A small gas pilot light that burns continuously is frequently used. Gas pilots usually have expanding gas valves that automatically increase flame size when motor circuit starts. After a fixed interval, the flame reverts to normal size.

c. Electric gas — An electric spark ignites a gas jet, which in turn ignites the oil air mixture.

d Oil pilot — A small oil flame is used.

e Manual — A burning wick or torch is placed in the combustion space through peepholes and thus ignites the charge. Operator should stand to one side of the fire door to guard against injury from chance explosion.

VI. Refractory

The refractory lining or material should be an insulating fireproof brick-like substance. Never use ordinary firebrick. The insulating brick should be set on end so as to build a 2 inch-thick wall in the pot. Size and shape of the refractory pot vary from furnace to furnace (see Figure 6 for various shapes). The shape can be either round or square, whichever is more convenient to build. It is important to use a special cement having properties similar to that of the insulating refractory-type brick.

VII. Heating Systems

A Steam Heating Systems - Steam heating systems are classified according to the pipe arrangement, accessories used, method of returning the con-densate to the boiler, method of expelling air from the system, or the type of control employed. The successful operation of a steam heating system consists of generating steam in sufficient quantity to equalize building heat loss at maximum efficiency, expelling entrapped air, and returning all condensate to the boiler rapidly. Steam cannot enter a space filled with air or water at pressure equal to the steam pressure. It is important, therefore, to eliminate air and to remove water from the distribution system. All hot pipe lines exposed to contact by residents must be properly insulated or guarded.

Steam heating systems are classified according to the method of returning the condensate to the boiler.

1 **Gravity One-pipe Air-vent System** — The gravity one-pipe air-vent system is one of the earliest types used. The condensate is returned to the boiler by gravity. This system is generally found in one-building-type heating systems. The steam is supplied by the boiler and carried through a single system or pipe to radiators as shown in Figure 7. Return of the condensate is dependent on hydrostatic head. Therefore, the end of the steam main, where it attaches to the boiler, must be full of water (termed a wet return) for a distance above the boiler line to create a pressure drop balance between the boiler and the steam main.

Radiators are equipped with an inlet valve and with an air valve (see Figure 8). The air valve permits venting of air from the radiator and its displacement by steam. Condensate is drained from the radiator through the same pipe that supplies steam.

2 **Two-pipe Steam Vapor System with Return Trap** — The two-pipe vapor system with boiler return trap and air eliminator is an improvement of the one-pipe system. The return connection of the radiator has a thermostatic trap that permits flow of condensate and air only from the radiator and prevents steam from leaving the radiator. Since the return main is at atmospheric pressure or less, a boiler return trap is installed to equalize condensate return pressure with boiler pressure.

B **Hot Water Heating Systems** — All hot water heating systems are similar in design and operating principle.

1 **One-pipe Gravity System** —The one-pipe gravity hot water heating system is the most elementary of the gravity systems and is shown in Figure 9. Water is heated at the lowest point in the system. It rises through a single main because of a difference in density between hot and cold water. The supply rise or radiator branch takes off from the top of the main to supply water to the radiators. After the water gives up heat in the radiator it goes back to the same main through return piping from the radiator. This cooler return water mixes with water in the supply main and causes the water to cool a little. As a result, the next radiator on the system has a lower emission rate and must be larger.

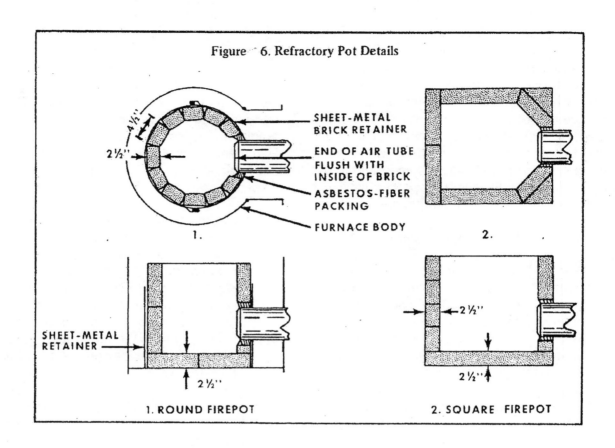

Figure 6. Refractory Pot Details

1. ROUND FIREPOT

2. SQUARE FIREPOT

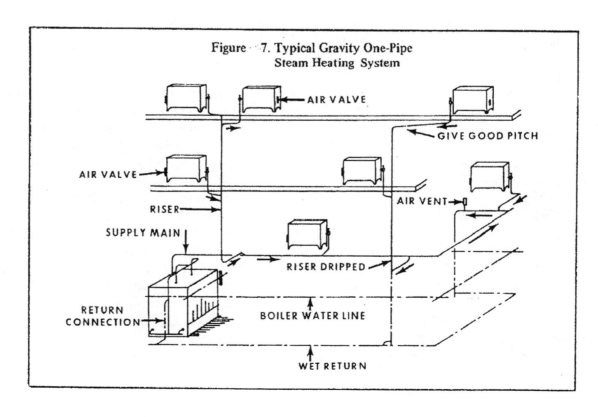

Figure 7. Typical Gravity One-Pipe
Steam Heating System

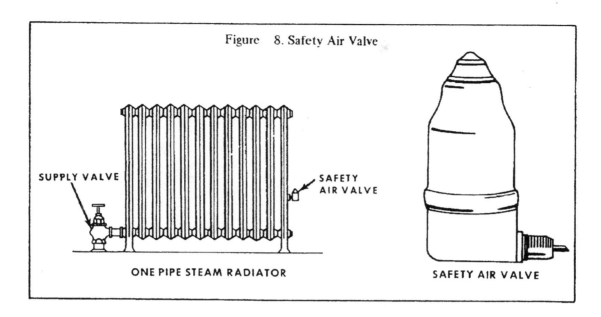

Figure 8. Safety Air Valve

SUPPLY VALVE

SAFETY AIR VALVE

ONE PIPE STEAM RADIATOR

SAFETY AIR VALVE

Note in Figure 9 that the high points of the hot water system are vented and the low points are drained. In this case, the radiators are the high points and the heater is the low point.

2 **One-pipe Forced-feed System** — If a pump or circulator is introduced in the main near the heater of the one-pipe system, we have a forced system that can be used for much larger

applications than the gravity type. This system can operate at higher water temperatures than the gravity system. The faster moving higher temperature water "Hakes a more responsive system with a smaller temperature drop through each radiator. Higher operating temperatures and lower temperature drops permit the use of smaller radiators for the same heating load.

3 **Two-pipe Gravity Systems** — One-pipe gravity systems may become a two-pipe system if the return radiator branch connects to a second main that returns water to the heater (see Figure 10). Water temperature is practically the same in all the radiators.

4 **Two-pipe Forced-circulation System** — This system is similar to a one-pipe forced-circulation system except that the same piping arrangement is found in the two-pipe gravity flow system.

5 **Expansion Tanks** — When water is heated it tends to expand. Therefore, in a hot water system an expansion tank is necessary. The expansion tank, either of open or closed type, must be of sufficient size to permit a change in water volume within the heating system. If the expansion tank is of the open type it must be placed at least 3 feet above the highest point of the system. It will require a vent and an overflow. The open tank is usually in an attic, where it needs protection from freezing.

The enclosed expansion tank is found in modern installations. An air cushion in the tank compresses and expands according to the change of volume and pressure in the system. Closed tanks are usually at the low point in the system and close to the heater. They can, however, be placed at almost any location within the heating system.

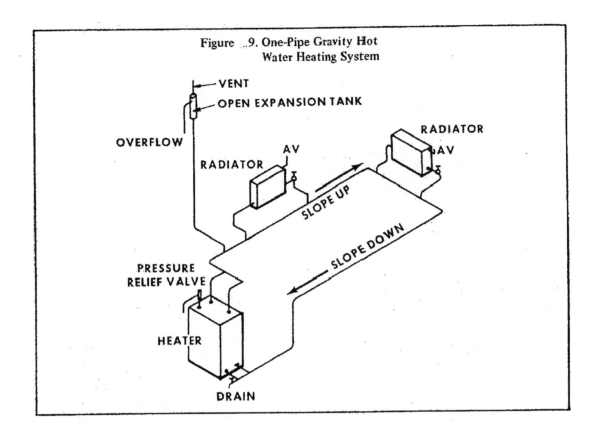

Figure 9. One-Pipe Gravity Hot Water Heating System

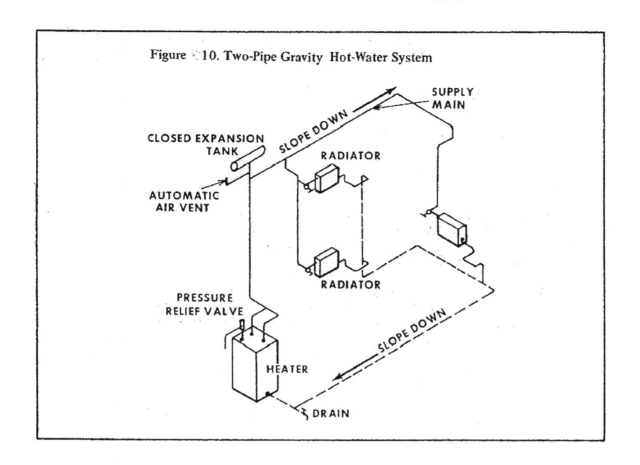

Figure 10. Two-Pipe Gravity Hot-Water System

SUPPLY MAIN

SLOPE DOWN

CLOSED EXPANSION TANK

RADIATOR

AUTOMATIC AIR VENT

RADIATOR

PRESSURE RELIEF VALVE

SLOPE DOWN

HEATER

DRAIN

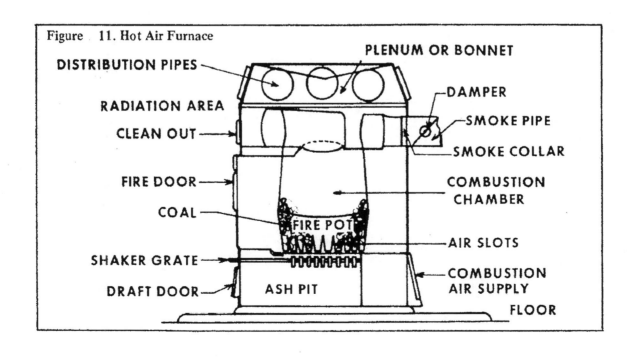

Figure 11. Hot Air Furnace

PLENUM OR BONNET

DISTRIBUTION PIPES

DAMPER

RADIATION AREA

SMOKE PIPE

CLEAN OUT

SMOKE COLLAR

FIRE DOOR

COMBUSTION CHAMBER

COAL

FIRE POT

AIR SLOTS

SHAKER GRATE

COMBUSTION AIR SUPPLY

DRAFT DOOR

ASH PIT

FLOOR

COAL NOTES

1. Approximately 12 pounds of air is required for complete combustion of 1 pound of hard coal.

2. Approximately 5 pounds of hard coal is consumed per hour for each square foot of grate area.

3. Approximately 12 inches of fire bed will heat most efficiently.

4. Anthracite coal burns more slowly than soft coal, is cleaner to handle-hence more widely used.

5. Large-size coal does not compact-hence the air spaces are too great and allows gases to escape into the flue unburned. Small size coal compacts too much and inhibits airflow through the coal to allow for good combustion. Mixing of coal size is recommended, i.e., stove and chestnut.

6. Fires burn best when the weather is clear and cold, because of reduced atmospheric pressure on the air in the flue—hence greater draft velocity. During periods of heavy atmosphere or rainy weather the temperature of flue gases must exceed normal temperatures to overcome the heavier atmospheric weight.

7. During extreme cold weather, coal should be added to a fire once in approximately 8 hours; moderate weather-12 hours.

C Hot Air Heating Systems

1 Gravity-Warm-Air Heating Systems — These operate because of the difference in specific gravity of warm air and cold air. Warm air is lighter than cold air and rises if cold air is available to replace it (see Figure 11).

a Operation — Satisfactory operation of a gravity-warm-air heating system depends on three factors. They are: (1) size of warm air and cold ducts, (2) heat loss of the building, (3) heat available from the furnace.

b Heat distribution — The most common source of trouble in these systems is insufficient pipe area usually in the return or cold air duct. The total cross-section area of the cold duct or ducts must be at least equal to the total cross-section area of all warm ducts.

c Pipeless furnaces — The pipeless hot-air furnace is the simplest type of hot-air furnace and is suitable for small homes where all rooms can be grouped about a single large register (see Figure 3). Other pipeless gravity furnaces are often installed at floor level. These are really oversized jacketed space heaters. The most common difficulty experienced with this type of furnace is supplying a return air opening of sufficient size on the floor.

2 Forced-Warm-Air Heating Systems — The mechanical warm-air furnace is the most modern type of warm-air equipment (see Figure 12). It is the safest type because it operates at low temperatures. The principle of a forced-warm-air heating system is very similar to that of the gravity system, except that a fan or blower is added to increase air movement. Because of the assistance of the fan or blower, the pitch of the ducts or leaders can be disregarded and it is therefore practical to deliver heated air in the most convenient places.

a Operation — In a forced-air system, operation of the fan or blower must be controlled by air temperature in a bonnet or by a blower control furnacestat. The blower control starts the fan or blower when the temperature reaches a certain point and turns the fan or blower off when the temperature drops to a predetermined point.

b Heat distribution — Dampers in the various warm-air ducts control distribution

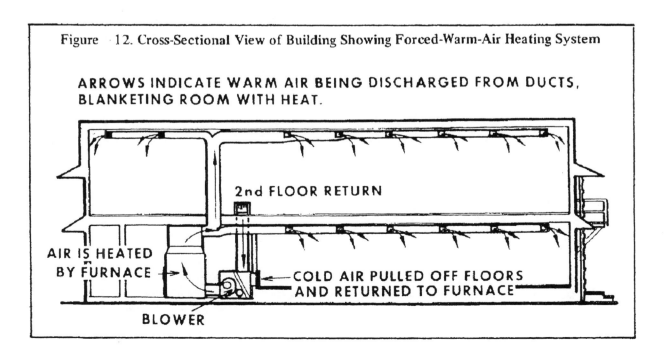

Figure 12. Cross-Sectional View of Building Showing Forced-Warm-Air Heating System

ARROWS INDICATE WARM AIR BEING DISCHARGED FROM DUCTS, BLANKETING ROOM WITH HEAT.

2nd FLOOR RETURN

AIR IS HEATED BY FURNACE

COLD AIR PULLED OFF FLOORS AND RETURNED TO FURNACE

BLOWER

of warm air either at the branch takeoff or at the warm-air outlet.

Humidifiers are often mounted in the supply bonnet in order to regulate the humidity within the residence.

D Space Heaters — Space unit heaters are the least desirable from the viewpoint of fire safety and housing inspection. All space unit heaters must be vented to the flue.

1 Coal-Fired Space Heaters (Cannon stove) — This is illustrated in Figure 13 and is made entirely of cast iron. In operation, coal on the grates receives primary air for combustion through the grates from the ash-door draft intake. Combustible gases driven from the coal by heat burn in the barrel of the stove, where they received additional or secondary air through the feed door. Side and top of the stove absorb the heat of combustion and radiate it to the surrounding space.

2 Oil-Fired Space Heaters — Oil-fired space heaters have atmospheric vaporizing-type burners. The burners require a light grade of fuel oil that vaporizes easily and is comparatively low in temperature. In addition, the oil must be such that it leaves only a small amount of carbon residue and ash within the heater. Oil-fired space heaters are basically of two types:

a Perforated-sleeve burner — The perforated-sleeve burner (see Figure 14) consists essentially of a metal base formed of two or more angular fuel-vaporizing bowl burners (see Figure 15) and is widely used in space heaters and some water heaters.

The burner consists essentially of a bowl, 8 to 13 inches in diameter, with perforations in the side that admit air for combustion. The upper part of the bowl has a flame ring or collar. When several space heaters are installed in a building, an oil supply from an

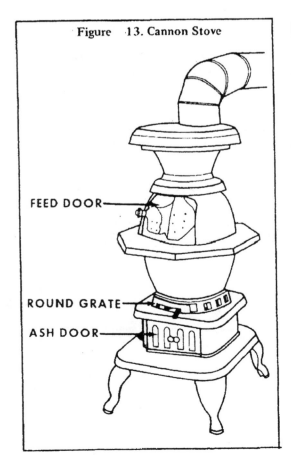

Figure 13. Cannon Stove

FEED DOOR

ROUND GRATE

ASH DOOR

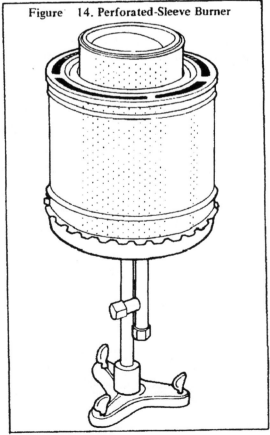

Figure 14. Perforated-Sleeve Burner

outside tank to all heaters is often desirable. Figure 16 shows the condition of a burner flame with different rates of fuel flow and indicates the ideal flame height.

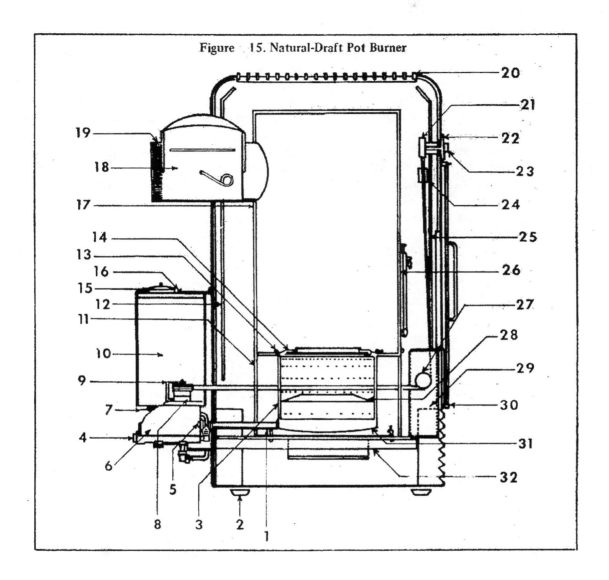

Figure 15. Natural-Draft Pot Burner

1 Burner-pot pipe.	12 Heat shield (rear).	22 Escutcheon plate.
2 Leg Leveler.	13 Burner-ring clamp.	23 Dial control knob.
3 Pilot-ring clip.	14 Burner-top ring.	24 Pulley assembly (short).
4 Strainer unit.	15 Fuel tank cap.	25 Heat shield (front).
5 Burner-pot drain plug.	16 Tank fuel gauge.	26 Heat-unit door.
6 Constant-level valve.	17 Heat unit.	27 Pulley assembly (long).
7 Tank valve	18 Cold draft regulator.	28 Pilot ring.
8 Control drum (to fit 6).	19 Flue connections, 6-inch	29 Humidifier.
9 Control pulley bracket	diameter.	30 Trim bar.
10 Fuel tank.	20 Top grille.	31 Burner pot.
11 Lower heat unit.	21 Dial control drum.	32 Heat-unit support.

3 Gas-Fired Space Heaters—There are three types of gas-fired space heaters: natural, manufactured, and liquified petroleum gas. Space heaters using natural, manufactured, or liquified petroleum gases have a similar construction. All gas-fired space heaters must be vented to prevent a dangerous buildup of poisonous gases.

Each unit console consists of an enamel steel cabinet with top and bottom circulating grilles or openings, gas burners, heating element, gas pilot, and gas valve (see Figure 17). The heating element or combustion chamber is usually cast iron.

CAUTION: All gas-fired space heaters and their connections must be of the type approved by the American Gas Association (AGA). They must be installed in accordance with the recommendations of that organization or the local code.

a Venting — Use of proper venting materials and correct installation of venting for gas-fired space heaters is necessary to minimize harmful effects of condensation and to ensure that combustion products are carried off. (Approximately 12 gallons of water are produced in the burning of 1,000 cubic feet of natural gas. The inner surface of the vent must therefore be heated above the dewpoint of the combustion products to prevent water. from forming in the flue.) A horizontal vent must be given an upward pitch of at least 1 inch per foot of horizontal distance.

When the smoke pipe extends through floors or walls the metal pipe must be insu-

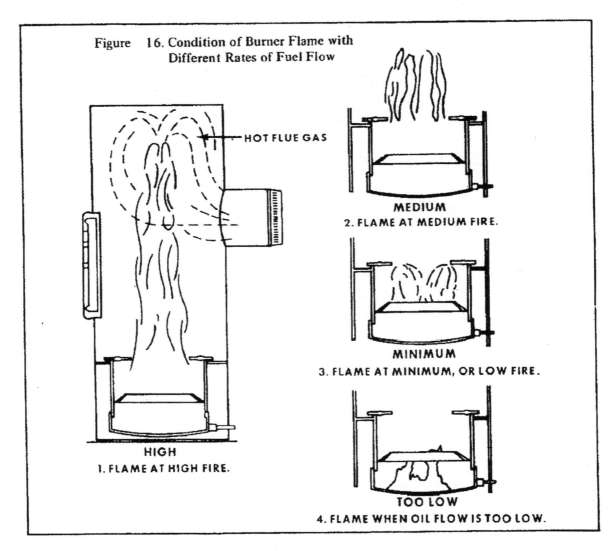

Figure 16. Condition of Burner Flame with Different Rates of Fuel Flow

HOT FLUE GAS

HIGH
1. FLAME AT HIGH FIRE.

MEDIUM
2. FLAME AT MEDIUM FIRE.

MINIMUM
3. FLAME AT MINIMUM, OR LOW FIRE.

TOO LOW
4. FLAME WHEN OIL FLOW IS TOO LOW.

lated from the floor or wall system by an air space (see Figure 18). Avoid sharp bends. A 90° vent elbow has a resistance to flow equivalent to a straight section of pipe having a length of 10 times the elbow diameter. Be sure vent is of a rigid construction and resistant to corrosion by flue gas products. Several types of venting material are available such as B-vent and several other ceramic-type materials. A chimney lined with fire-brick type of terra cotta must be relined with an acceptable vent material if it is to be used for venting gas-fired appliances.

Use the same size vent pipe throughout its length. Never make a vent smaller than heater outlet except when two or more vents converge from separate heaters. To determine the size of vents beyond the point of convergence, add one-half the area of each vent to the area of the largest heater's vent.

Figure 17. Typical Gas-Fired Space Heater

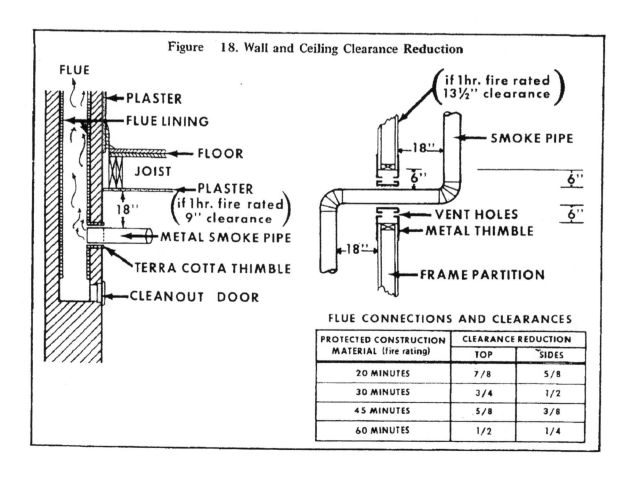

Figure 18. Wall and Ceiling Clearance Reduction

FLUE CONNECTIONS AND CLEARANCES

PROTECTED CONSTRUCTION MATERIAL (fire rating)	CLEARANCE REDUCTION	
	TOP	SIDES
20 MINUTES	7/8	5/8
30 MINUTES	3/4	1/2
45 MINUTES	5/8	3/8
60 MINUTES	1/2	1/4

Install vents with male ends of inner liner down to ensure condensate is kept within pipes on a cold start. The vertical length of each vent or stack should be at least 2 feet greater than the length between horizontal connection and stack.

Run vent at least 3 feet above any projection of the building within 20 feet to place it above a possible pressure zone due to wind currents (see Figure 19). End it with a weather cap designed to prevent entrance of rain and snow.

Gas-fired space heaters as well as gas furnaces and hot water heaters must be equipped with a backdraft diverter (see Figure ,20) designed to protect heaters against downdrafts and excessive updrafts. Use only draft diverters of the type approved by the AGA.

The combustion chamber or firebox must be insulated from the floor, usually with an air-space of 15 to 18 inches, or the firebox is sometimes insulated within the unit and thus allows for lesser clearance for combustibles.

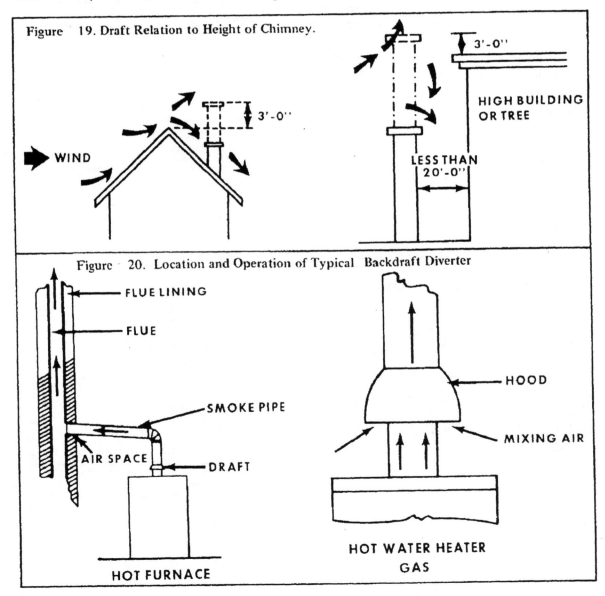

Figure 19. Draft Relation to Height of Chimney.

3'-0"

HIGH BUILDING OR TREE

3'-0"

WIND

LESS THAN 20'-0"

Figure 20. Location and Operation of Typical Backdraft Diverter

FLUE LINING

FLUE

SMOKE PIPE

AIR SPACE

DRAFT

HOOD

MIXING AIR

HOT FURNACE

HOT WATER HEATER GAS

Where coal space heaters are located, a floor protection should be provided. This would be a metal-covered asbestos board or a similar durable insulation material. One reason for the floor protection would be to allow cooling off of hot coals and ashes if they drop out while ashes are being removed from the ash chamber. Walls and ceilings of a non-combustible construction exposed to furnace radiation should be installed, and the following clearances are recommended: Space heaters — A top or ceiling clearance of 36 inches, a wall clearance of 18 inches, and a smoke pipe clearance of 18 inches, (see Figure 18).

VIII. Domestic Hot Water Jack Stoves (Coal Stoves)

Domestic hot water jack stoves (coal stoves) equipped with water jackets to supply hot water for domestic use are to be treated as coal-fired furnaces or boilers previously discussed. Note that flue connections should not exceed two to the same flue unless the draft and size are sufficient to accommodate both exhausting requirements. One flue with one smoke pipe is the rule; however, housing inspectors may find a jack stove and main furnace connected to the same flue. Where these conditions are encountered and no complaint about malfunctioning of this system is found, it can be assumed that the system is operating satisfactorily. Where more than two units, other than gas, are attached to a single flue, the building agency should be notified, since this can be considered an improper installation. Gas, oil, and electric hot water heating units for domestic hot water should be treated the same as previously discussed for central heating units.

IX. Hazardous Installations

A **Generalities** — The housing inspector should be on the alert for unvented open burning flame heaters, such as manually operated gas logs. Coil-type wall-mounted hot-water heaters that do not have safety relief valves are not permitted. Kerosene (portable) units for cooking or heating should be prohibited. Generally, open-flame portable units are not allowed under fire safety regulations.

In oil heating units, other than integral tank units, the oil filling and vent must be located on the exterior of the building. Filling of oil within buildings is prohibited.

Electric wiring to heating units must be installed as indicated in the electrical section. Cutoff switches should be close to the entry but outside of the boiler room. The inspector should be able to appraise the heating installation and determine its adequacy. Any installation that indicates haphazard location, workmanship, or operation, whether it be building, zoning, plumbing, electrical, or housing, will dictate further inspection.

B **Chimneys (see Figure 21 and 22)** - Chimneys, as all inspectors know, are an integral part of the building. The chimney is a point of building safety and should be understood by the housing inspector. The chimney, if of masonry, must be tight and sound; flues should be terra cotta lined, and where no linings are installed, the brick should be tight to permit proper draft and elimination of combustion gases.

Chimneys that act as flues for gas-fired equipment must be lined with either B-vent or terra cotta.

To the inspector, on exterior inspection, "banana peel" on the portion of the chimney above the roof will indicate trouble and a need for rebuilding. Exterior deterioration of the chimney will, if let go too long, gradually permit erosion from within the flues and eventually block the flue opening.

Rusted flashing at the roof level will also contribute to the chimney's deterioration. Effervescence on the inside wall of the chimney below the roof and on the outside of the chimney, if exposed, will show salt accumulations — a tell-tale sign of water penetration and flue gas escape and a sign of chimney deterioration. In the spring and fall, during rain seasons, if terra cotta chimneys leak, the joint will be indicated by dark areas permitting actual counting of the number of flues inside the masonry chimney. When this condition occurs, it usually requires 2 or 3 months to dry out. Upon drying out, the mortar joints are discolored (brown), and so after a few years of this type of deterioration the joints can be distinguished wet or dry. The above-listed conditions usually develop during coal operation and become more pronounced usually 2 to 5 years after conversion to oil or gas.

An unlined chimney can be checked for deterioration below the roof line by checking the residue deposited at the base of the chimney, usually accessible through a clea-nout (door or plug) or breaching. Red gran-ular or fine powder showing through coal soot or oil soot will generally indicate, if in quantity (a handful), that deterioration is excessive and repairs are needed.

Gas units attached to unlined chimneys will be devoid of soot, but will usually show similar tell-tale brick powder and deterioration as previously mentioned. Manufactured gas has a greater tendency to dehydrate and decompose brick in chimney flues than natural gas. For gas installations in older homes, utility companies usually specify chimney requirements before installation, and so older chimneys may require the installation of terra cotta liners, lead-lined copper liners,

or transite pipe. Oil burner operation using a low air ratio and high oil consumption is usually indicated by black carbon deposits around the top of the chimney. Prolonged operation in this burner setting results in long carbon water deposits down the chimney for 4 to 6 feet or more and should indicate to the inspector a possibility of poor burner maintenance. This will accent his need to be more thorough on the ensuing inspection. This type of condition can result from other related causes, such as improper chimney height or exterior obstructions such as trees or buildings that will cause downdrafts or insufficient draft or contribute to a faulty heating operation. Rust spots and soot-mold usually occur on galvanized smoke pipe deterioration.

C Fireplace — Careful attention should be given to the construction of the fireplace. Improperly built fireplaces are a serious safety and fire hazard (see Figure 22). The most common causes of fireplace fires are thin walls, combustible materials such as studding or trim against sides and back of the fireplace, wood mantels, and unsafe hearths.

Fireplace walls should be not less than 8 inches thick, and if built of stone or hollow masonry units, not less than 12 inches thick. The faces of all walls exposed to fire should be lined with firebrick or other suitable fire-resistive material. When the lining consists of 4 inches of firebrick, such lining thickness may be included in the required minimum thickness of the wall.

The fireplace hearth should be constructed of brick, stone, tile, or similar incombustible material and should be supported on a fireproof slab or on a brick arch. The hearth should extend at least 20 inches beyond the chimney breast and not less than 12 inches beyond each side of the fireplace opening

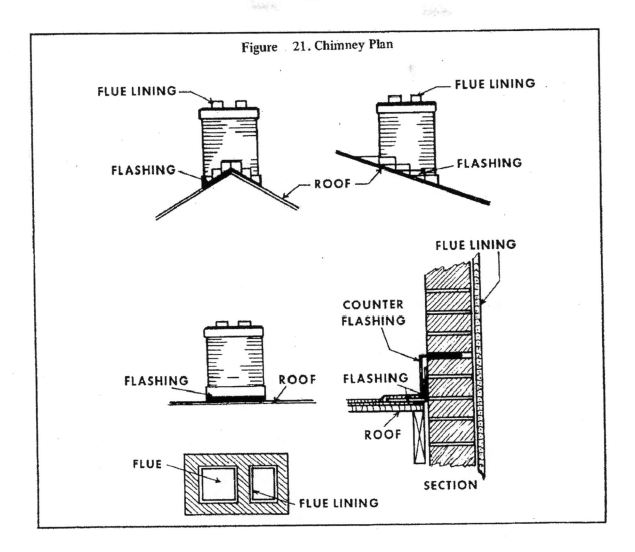

Figure 21. Chimney Plan

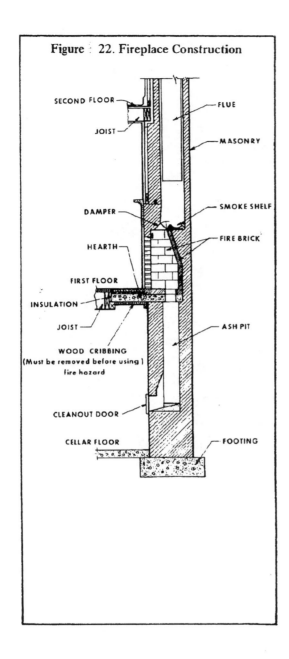

Figure 22. Fireplace Construction

SECOND FLOOR

FLUE

JOIST

MASONRY

DAMPER

SMOKE SHELF

HEARTH

FIRE BRICK

FIRST FLOOR

INSULATION

JOIST

ASH PIT

WOOD CRIBBING
(Must be removed before using)
fire hazard

CLEANOUT DOOR

CELLAR FLOOR

FOOTING

along the chimney breast. The combined thickness of the hearth and its supporting construction should be not less than 6 inches at any point.

It is important that all wooden beams, joists, and studs are set off from the fireplace and chimney so that there is not less than 2 inches of clearance between the wood members and the sidewalls of the fireplace or chimney and not less than 4 inches of clearance between wood members and the back wall of the fireplace.

The housing inspector is a very important person in maintaining sound, safe, and healthful community growth. This should be a challenge to every inspector to provide himself with the necessary tools for better and more efficient housing inspection. He must develop the extra senses so necessary in spotting and correcting faults. He must know when to refer and to whom the referral is to be made; he must be continually seeking knowledge, which may be found by consulting with technicians, tradesmen, and professionals. No finer satisfaction can be realized than to know and feel that the security, safety, and comfort of each and every family within your community has a better and more healthful life because of that extra bit of knowledge you have imparted. "An inspector who stops learning today is uneducated tomorrow."

GLOSSARY OF ENGINEERING TERMS

TABLE OF CONTENTS

GLOSSARY OF ENGINEERING TERMS

ABT (AUTOMATIC BUS TRANSFER): An automatic electrical device that supplies power to vital equipment. This device will shift from the normal power supply to an alternate power supply when the normal supply is interrupted.

ACETYLENE: A gas that is chemically produced from calcium carbide and water, used for welding and cutting.

ADAPTER: A coupling or similar device that permits fittings with different-sized openings (apertures) to be joined together.

AIR EJECTOR: A type of jet pump, used to remove air and other gases from the condensers.

AIR CHAMBER: A chamber, usually bulb-shaped, on the suction and discharge sides of a pump. Air in the chamber acts as a cushon and prevents sudden shocks to the pump.

AIR REGISTER: A device in the casing of a boiler, used for regulating the amount of air for combustion and to provide a circular motion to the air.

AISE: Association of Iron and Steel Engineers.

ALLOY: A mixture composed of two or more metals.

ALTERNATING CURRENT (A-C): Current that is constantly changing in value and direction at regular recurring intervals.

AMBIENT TEMPERATURE: The temperature of the surrounding area.

AMMETER: An instrument for measuring the rate of flow of electrical current in amperes.

ANNEALING: The softening of metal by heating and slow cooling.

ANNUNCIATOR: See ENGINE ORDER TELEGRAPH.

ARGON: An inert gas, slightly heavier than air, used in inert-gas shielded metal arc welding.

ARMORED CABLE: An electric cable that is protected on the outside by a metal covering.

ASTM: American Society for Testing Metals.

AUTOMATIC COMBUSTION CONTROL SYSTEM (ACC): A system that provides a means of automatically controlling the fuel and air mixture in a boiler.

BACK PRESSURE: The pressure exerted on the exhaust side of a pump or engine.

BDC (BOTTOM DEAD CENTER): The position of a reciprocating piston at its lowest point of travel.

BALLASTING: The process of filling empty tanks with salt water, to protect the ship from underwater damage and increase its stability. See DEBALLASTING.

BLUEPRINTS: Reproduced copies of drawings (usually having white lines on a blue background.

BOILER: A strong' metal tank or vessel composed of tubes, drums, and headers, in which water is heated by the gases of combustion to form steam.

BOILER CENTRAL CONTROL STATION: A centrally located station for directing the control of all boilers in the fireroom.

BOILER DESIGN PRESSURE: Pressure specified by the manufacturer, usually about 103% of normal steam drum operating pressure.

BOILER INTERNAL FITTINGS: All parts inside the boiler which control the flow of steam and water.

BOILER OPERATING PRESSURE: The pressure required to be maintained in a boiler while in service.

BOILER OPERATING STATION: A location from which boilers are operated.

BOILER RECORD SHEET: A NavShips form maintained for each boiler, which serves as a monthly summary of operation.

BOILER REFRACTORIES: Materials used in the boiler furnace to protect the boiler from heat of combustion.

BOILER ROOM: A compartment containing boilers but not containing a station for operating or firing the boilers. Refers specifically to bulkhead enclosed boiler installations.

BOILER TUBE CLEANER: A CYLINDRICAL brush that is used to clean the insides of boiler tubes.

BOILER WATER: Refers to the water actually contained in the boiler.

BRAZING: A method of joining two metals at high temperature with a molten alloy.

BRINE: A highly concentrated solution of salt in water, normally associated with the overboard discharge of distilling plants.

BRITTLENESS: That property of a material which causes it to fracture prior to any noticeable signs of deformation.

BURNERMAN: Man in fireroom who tends the burners in the boilers.

BUSHING: A renewable lining for a hole through which a moving part passes.

BYPASS: To divert the flow of gas or liquid. Also, the line that diverts the flow.

CALIBRATION: The comparison of any measuring instrument with a set standard.

CANTILEVER: A projecting arm or beam supported only at one end.

CAPILLARY TUBE: A slender thin-walled small-bored tube used with remote-reading indicators.

CARBON DIOXIDE: A colorless, orderless gas used as a fire extinguishing agent and for inflating liferafts and lifejackets.

CARBON PACKING: Pressed segments of graphite used to prevent steam leakage around shafts.

CASUALTY POWER SYSTEM: A means of using portable cables to transmit power to vital equipment in an emergency.

CHECK VALVE: A valve that permits a flow of liquid in one direction only.

CHILL SHOCKING: A method of removing scale from the tubes of a distilling plant, utilizing steam and cold water.

CHLORINE: A heavy gas, greenish-yellow in color used for water purification, sewage disposal, and in the preparation of bleaching solutions. Poisonous in concentrated form.

CIRCUIT BREAKER: An electrical device that provides circuit overload protection.

CLUTCH: A form of coupling which is designed to connect or disconnect a driving or driven member.

COMPARTMENT CHECKOFF LIST: A list of all damage control fittings, their location, and status for different ship conditions.

CONDENSER: A heat transfer device in which steam or vapor is condensed to water.

CONDUCTION: A method of heat transfer from one body to another when the two bodies are in physical contact.

CONSTANT PRESSURE GOVERNOR: A device that maintains a constant pump discharge pressure under varying loads.

CONTROLLER: A device used to stop, start, and protect motors from overloads, while they are running.

CORROSION: The process of being eaten away gradually by chemical action, such as rusting.

COUNTERSINK: A cone-shaped tool used to enlarge and bevel one end of a drilled hole.

CROSS-CONNECTED PLANT: A method of operating two or more plants as one unit, having a common steam supply.

CURTIS STAGE: A velocity-compounded impulse turbine stage having one pressure drop in the nozzles and two velocity drops in the blading.

DEAERATING FEED TANK (DA TANK): A unit in the steam-water cycle used to (1) free the condensate of dissolved oxygen, (2) heat the feed water, and (3) act as a reservoir for feed water.

DEBALLASTING: The process of emptying salt from tanks, to protect the ship from underwater damage and increase its stability.

DEGREE OF SUPERHEAT: The amount by which the temperature of steam exceeds saturation temperature.

DIATOMACEOUS EARTH: A light, crumbly silica material derived from algae and microscopic skeletons. It has relatively high absorption and filtering qualities.

DIATOMITE FILTERS: Filters made of a diatomaceous earth and asbestos filler.

DIRECT CURRENT (D-C): Current that moves in one direction only.

DIRECT DRIVE: One in which the drive mechanism is coupled directly to the driven member.

DISTILLATE: Fresh water produced in distilling plants.

DISTILLING PLANTS: Units commonly called evaporators (evaps) used to convert seawater into fresh water.

DRAWING: The plans used to show the fabrication and assembly details.

DRUM, STEAM: The large tank at the top of the boiler in which the steam collects.

DRUM, WATER: A tank at the bottom of a boiler; also called MUD DRUM.

DRY PIPE: A perforated pipe at the highest point in a steam drum to collect steam.

DUCTILITY: Property possessed by metals that allows them to be drawn or stretched.

ECONOMIZER: A heat transfer device on a boiler that uses the gases of combustion to preheat the feed water.

EDUCTOR: A jet type pump (no moving parts) used to empty flooded spaces.

EFFICIENCY: The ratio of the output to the input.

ELASTICITY: The ability of a material to return to its original size and shape.

ELECTRODE: A metallic rod (welding rod) used in electric welding that melts when current is passed through it.

ELECTROHYDRAULIC STEERING: A system having a motor-driven hydraulic pump that creates the force needed to actuate the rams to position the ship's rudder.

ELECTROLYSIS: A chemical action that takes place between unlike metals in systems using salt water.

ELECTROMOTIVE FORCE (EMF): A force that causes electrons to move through a closed circuit; expressed in volts.

ELEMENT: A substance which consists of chemically united atoms of one kind.

ENERGY: The capacity for doing work.

ENGINEER'S BELL BOOK: A legal record maintained by the throttle watch of all ordered main engine speed changes.

ENGINE ORDER TELEGRAPH: A device on the ship's bridge to give orders to the engine-room. Also called ANNUNCIATOR.

EPM (EQUIVALENTS PER MILLION): The number of equivalent parts of a substance per million parts of another substance. The word "equivalent" refers to the equivalent weight of a substance.

EXPANSION JOINT: A junction which allows for expansion and contraction.

FATIGUE: The tendency of a material to break under repeated strain.

FEED HEATER: A heat transfer device used to heat the feed water before it goes to the boiler.

FEED WATER: Fresh water, with the highest possible level of purity, made in EVAPORATORS for use in boilers.

FERROUS METAL: Metal with a high iron content.

FIREBOX: The section of a ship's boiler where fuel oil combustion takes place.

FIREMAIN: The salt water line that provides fire-fighting and flushing water throughout the ship.

FIRE TUBE BOILER: Boilers in which the gases of combustion pass through the tubes and heat the water surrounding them.

FLAREBACK: A backfire of flame and hot gases into a ship's fireroom from the firebox. Caused by a fuel oil explosion in the firebox.

FLASH POINT OF OIL: That temperature at which the oil vapor will flash into fire but the main body of the oil will not ignite.

FLEXIBLE I-BEAM: An I-shaped steel beam on which the forward end of a turbine is mounted; it allows for longitudinal expansion and contraction.

FLOOR PLATES: The removable deck plating of a fireroom or engineroom aboard ship.

FLUX: A chemical agent that retards oxidation of the surface, removes oxides already present, and aids fusion.

FORCE: Anything that tends to produce or modify motion.

FORCED DRAFT: A term used to describe air under pressure supplied to the burners in a ship's boiler.

FORCED DRAFT BLOWERS: Turbine-driven fans which supply air to the boiler furnace.

FORCED FEED LUBRICATION: A lubrication system that uses a pump to maintain a constant pressure.

FORGING: The forming of metal by heating and hammering.

FRESH WATER SYSTEM: A piping system which supplies fresh water throughout the ship.

FUEL OIL MICROMETER VALVE: A valve installed at the burner manifold, which is used to control the fuel oil pressure to the burners.

FUEL OIL SERVICE TANKS: Tanks from which the fuel oil service pumps take suction for discharging oil to the burners.

FUSE: A protective device that is designed to open a circuit if the current flow exceeds a predetermined value.

GAGE GLASS: A device for indicating the liquid level in a tank.

GAS-FREE: A term used to describe a space that has been tested and found safe for hot work (welding & cutting).

GEARED-TURBINE DRIVE: A turbine that drives a pump, generator, or other machinery through reduction gears.

GROUNDED PLUG: A three pronged electrical plug used for grounding portable tools to the ship's structure. It is a safety device which always must be checked prior to using portable tools.

HAGEVAP SOLUTION: A chemical compound used in distilling plants, to prevent the formation of scale.

HALIDE LEAK DETECTOR: A device that is used to locate leaks in refrigeration systems.

HANDHOLE: An opening that is large enough for the hand and arm to enter the boiler for making slight repairs, and for inspection.

HANDY BILLY: A small portable water pump.

HARDENING: The heating and rapid cooling (quenching) of metal to induce hardness.

HARDNESS: The ability of a material to resist penetration.

HEAT EXCHANGER: Any device that is designed to allow the transfer of heat from one fluid (liquid or gas) to another.

HYDROGEN: A highly explosive, light, invisible, non-poisonous gas used for underwater welding and cutting operations.

HYDROMETER: An instrument used for determining the specific gravity of liquids.

HYDROSTATIC TEST: A pressure test using water to detect leaks in a boiler or other closed systems.

IGNITION, COMPRESSION: Ignition where the heat generated by compression in an internal combustion engine ignites the fuel (as in a diesel engine).

IGNITION, SPARK: Ignition where the mixture of air and fuel in an internal combustion-engine is ignited by an electric spark (as in a gasoline engine).

IMPELLER: An encased, rotating element provided with vanes which draw in fluid at the center and expel it at a high velocity at the outer edge.

IMPULSE TURBINE: A turbine in which the major part of the driving force is received from the impulse of incoming steam.

INDIRECT DRIVE: A drive mechanism coupled to the driven member by gears or belts.

INERT: Inactive.

INJECTOR: A device which, by means of a jet of steam, forces water into the boiler, or as in the diesel engineforces fuel into the cylinders.

INSULATION: A material used to retard heat transfer.

JACKBOX: Receptacle, usually secured to a bulkhead, in which telephone jacks are mounted.

JOB ORDER: The order issued by a repair activity to its own subdivisions, to perform a repair job in response to a WORK REQUEST.

JUMPER: Any connecting pipe, hose, or wire, normally for use in emergencies aboard ship, used to bypass damaged sections of a pipe, a hose, or & wire. (See BYPASS.)

JURY RIG: Any temporary or makeshift device.

LABYRINTH PACKING: Rows of metallic strips or fins used to prevent steam leakage along the shaft or a turbine.

LAGGING: A protective and confining cover placed over insulating material.

LIGHT OFF: Start, literally; 'to start a fire in," as in "light off a boiler."

LOG BOOK: Any chronological record of events, such as an engineering watch log.

LOG, ENGINEERING: A legal record of important events and data concerning the machinery of a ship.

LOG ROOM: Engineer's office on board ship.

LUBE OIL PURIFIER: A unit that removes water and sediment from lubricating oil by centrifugal force.

MACHINABILITY: The term used to describe the ease with which a metal may be turned, planed, milled, or otherwise shaped.

MAIN CONDENSER: A heat exchanger which converts exhaust steam to feed water.

MAIN DRAIN SYSTEM: The system used for pumping bilges, consisting of pumps and associated piping.

MAKEUP FEED: Water of required purity intended for use in ship's boilers. It is the water needed to replace that lost in the steam cycle.

MALLEABILITY: That property of a material which enables it to be stamped, hammered, or rolled into thin sheets.

MANIFOLD: A fitting with numerous branches used to convey fluids between a large pipe and several smaller pipes.

MECHANICAL ADVANTAGE (MA): The advantage (leverage) gained by the use of such devices as a wheel to open a large valve, chain falls and block and tackle to lift heavy weights, and wrenches to tighten nuts on bolts.

MECHANICAL CLEANING: A method of cleaning the firesides of boilers by scraping and wire-brushing.

MICROMHOS: Electrical units used with salinity indicators for measuring the conductivity of water.

MOTOR GENERATOR SET: A machine which consists of a motor mechanically coupled to a generator and usually mounted on the same base.

NAVY BOILER COMPOUND: A powdered chemical mixture used in boiler water treatment to convert scale-forming salts into sludge.

NAVY SPECIAL FUEL OIL (NSFO): The name applied to the grade of fuel oil that the Navy uses in combatant ships.

NIGHT ORDER BOOK: A notebook containing standing and special instructions by the engineer officer to the night engineering officer of the watch.

NITROGEN: An inert gas which will not support life or combustion. Used in recoil systems and other spaces requiring an inert atmosphere.

NONFERROUS METAL: Metals that are composed primarily of some element or elements other than iron.

OFFICER OF THE WATCH (OOW): Officer on duty in the engineering spaces.

OIL KING: A petty officer who receives, transfers, discharges, and tests fuel oil and maintains fuel oil records.

OIL POLLUTION ACTS: The Oil Pollution Act of 1924 (as amended) and the Oil Pollution Act of 1961 prohibit the overboard discharge of oil and water containing oil in port, in any sea area within 50 miles of land, and in special prohibited zones.

ORIFICE: A small opening.

OVERLOAD RELAY: An electrical protective device which automatically trips when a circuit draws excessive current.

OXIDATION: The process of various elements and compounds combining with oxygen. The corrosion of metals is generally a form of oxidation; rust on iron, for example, is iron oxide or oxidation.

PANT, PANTING: A series of pulsations caused by minor, recurrent explosions in the firebox of a ship's boiler. Usually caused by a shortage of air.

PERIPHERY: The curved line which forms the boundary of a circle (circumference), ellipse, or similar figure.

PITOMETER LOG: Device for indicating speed of ship and distance traveled by measuring water pressure on a tube projected outside the ship's hull.

PLASTICITY: That property which enables a material to be excessively and permanently deformed without breaking.

PNEUMERCATOR: A type of manometer used for measuring the volume of liquid in tanks.

PPM (PARTS PER MILLION): A comparison of the number of parts of a substance in a million parts of another substance. Used to measure the salt content of water.

PREHEATING: The application of heat to the base metal prior to a welding or cutting operation.

PRIME MOVER: The source of motion as a turbine, automobile engine, etc.

PUNCHING TUBES: The name applied to the mechanical means of cleaning the interiors of boiler tubes.

RADIATION, HEAT: The process of emitting heat in the form of heat waves.

REACH RODS: A length of pipe or back stock used as an extension on valve stems.

REACTION TURBINE: A turbine in which the major part of the driving force is received from the reactive force of steam leaving the blading.

REDUCER: Any coupling or fitting which connects a large opening to a smaller pipe or hose.

REDUCING VALVES: Automatic valves which are used to provide a steady pressure lower than the supply pressure.

REDUCTION GEAR: A set of gears used to transmit the rotation of one shaft to another at a slower speed.

REEFER: A provision cargo ship or a refrigerated compartment. An authorized abbreviation for refrigerator.

REFRIGERANT 12 (R-12): A nonpoisonous gas that is used in air conditioning and refrigeration systems.

REGULATOR (GAS): An instrument used to control the flow of gases from compressed gas cylinders.

REMOTE OPERATING GEAR: Flexible cables attached to valve wheels which permit the valves to be operated from another compartment.

RISER: A vertical pipe leading off a larger one; e.g., fireman riser.

ROOT VALVE: A valve located where a branch line comes off the main line.

ROTARY SWITCH: An electrical switch which closes or opens the circuit by a rotating motion.

SAE: Society of Automotive Engineers.

SAFETY VALVES: An automatic, quick opening and closing valve which has a reseat-pressure lower than the lift pressure.

SALINOMETER: A hydrometer that measures the concentration of salt in a solution.

SATURATION PRESSURE: The pressure corresponding to the saturation temperature.

SATURATION TEMPERATURE: The temperature at which a liquid boils under a given pressure. For any given saturation temperature there is a corresponding saturation pressure.

SCALE: Undesirable deposit, mostly calcium sulfate, which forms in the tubes of boilers.

SENTINEL VALVES: Small relief valves used primarily as a warning device.

SHAFT ALLEY: The long compartment of a ship in which the propeller shafts revolve.

SKETCH: A rough drawing indicating major features of an object to be constructed.

SLIDING FEET: A mounting for turbines and boilers to allow for expansion and contraction.

SLUDGE: The sediment left in fuel oil tanks.

SOLID COUPLING: A device used to join two shafts rigidly.

SOOT BLOWER: A soot removal device using a steam jet to clean the firesides of a boiler.

SPECIFIC HEAT: The amount of heat required to raise the temperature of one gram of a substance $1^{\circ}C$. All substances are compared to water which has a specific heat of 1.

SPEED-LIMITING GOVERNOR: A device for limiting the rotational speed of a prime mover.

SPEED-REGULATING GOVERNOR: A device that maintains a constant speed on a piece of machinery that is operating under varying load conditions.

SPLIT PLANT: A method of operating propulsion plants so that they are divided into two or more separate and complete units.

SPRING BEARINGS: Bearings positioned at various intervals along a propulsion shaft to help keep it in alignment and support its weight.

SPRINKLING SYSTEM: An automatic watering system used for cooling and flooding magazines and cargo spaces in case of fire.

STATIC: A force exerted by reason of weight alone, related to bodies at rest or in balance.

STEAM LANCE: A device for using low pressure steam inside of boilers to remove soot and carbon from boiler tubes.

STEERING ENGINE: The machinery that turns the rudder.

STERN TUBE: A watertight enclosure for the propeller shaft.

STRAIN: The deformation or change in shape of a material resulting from the applied load.

STRENGTH: The ability of a material to resist strain.

STRESS: Force producing or tending to produce deformation of a metal.

STUFFING BOX: A device to prevent leakage between a moving and a fixed part in a steam engineering plant.

STUFFING TUBE: A packed tube making a watertight fitting through a bulkhead for a cable or small pipe.

SUMP: A container, compartment, or reservoir; used as a drain or receptacle for fluids.

SUPERHEATER: A unit in the boiler that drys the steam and raises its temperature.

SWASH PLATES: Metal plates in the lower part of the steam drum that prevent the surging of boiler water with the motion of the ship.

SWITCHBOARD: A panel or group of panels with automatic protective devices, used to distribute the electrical power throughout the ship.

TANK TOP: Top side of tank section or double bottom of a ship.

TDC (TOP DEAD CENTER): The position of a reciprocating piston at its uppermost point of travel.

TEMPERING: The heating and controlled cooling of a metal to produce the desired hardness.

THIEF SAMPLE: A sample of oil or water taken from a ship's tank for analysis.

THROTTLEMAN: Man in the engineroom who operates the throttles to control the main engines.

THRUST BEARING: A bearing designed to limit the end play and absorb the axial thrust of a shaft.

TO BLOW TUBES: A procedure, using steam, for removing soot and carbon from the tubes of steaming boilers.

TOP OFF: To fill up, as a ship tops off in fuel oil before leaving port.

TOUGHNESS: That property of a material which enables it to withstand shock, and to be deformed without breaking.

TRANSFORMER: An electrical device used to step up or step down an a-c voltage.

TRICK WHEEL: A steering wheel in the steering engineroom or emergency steering station of a ship.

TUBE EXPANDER: A tool used to expand replacement tubes into their seats in boiler drums and headers.

TURBINE: A multibladed rotor, driven by steam or hot gas.

TURBINE JACKING GEAR: A motor-driven gear arrangement used to slowly rotate idle propulsion shafts and turbines.

TURBINE STAGE: The term applied to one set of nozzles and the succeeding row or rows of moving blades.

UPTAKES (EXHAUST TRUNKS): Large enclosed passages for exhaust gases from boilers to the stacks.

VENT: A valve in a tank or compartment used primarily to permit air to escape.

VENTURI INJECTOR: A device used for washing the firesides of boilers.

VOID: A small empty compartment below decks.

VOLATILE: The term used to describe a liquid that vaporizes quickly.

VOLTAGE TESTER (WIGGINS): A portable instrument that is used to detect electricity.

WATER TUBE BOILER: Boilers in which the water flows through the tubes and is heated by the gases of combustion.

WATER WASHING: A method of cleaning the firesides of boilers to remove soot and carbon.

WELDING LEAD: The conductor through which the electrical current is transmitted from the power source to the electrode holder and welding rod.

WHELPS: Any of the ribs or ridges on the barrel of a capstan or windlass.

WIREWAYS: Passageways, between decks and on the overheads of compartments, that contain electric cables.

WORK REQUEST: Request issued to a naval shipyard, tender, or repair ship for repairs.

ZERK FITTING: A small fitting to which a grease gun can be applied to force lubricating grease into bearings or moving parts of machinery.

ZINC: A metal placed in salt water systems to counteract the effects of electrolysis.